D1352149

PRIVATISATION?

PRIVATISATION?

Edited by

Sue Hastings
and Hugo Levie

with a foreword by Rodney Bickerstaffe

Spokesman

First published in Great Britain in 1983 by Spokesman
Bertrand Russell House, Gamble Street, Nottingham NG7 4ET

This book is copyright under the Berne Convention.
No part of this publication may be reproduced or transmitted in
any form or by any means without permission.

Copyright © Spokesman

Privatisation?
1. Government ownership — Great Britain
2. Municipal ownership — Great Britain
I. Hastings, Sue   II. Levie, Hugo
363'.0941   HD4645.AI

ISBN 0-85124-395-2
ISBN 0-85124-360-6 Pbk

Cover photo by Carlos Augusto (IFL)
Printed by the Russell Press Ltd., Nottingham

Contents

Foreword

Keep Our Services Public

Amongst the tactics used by the present Conservative Government to attack British workers, privatisation is perhaps the most venomous. Privatisation increases unemployment, reduces the standard of living and working conditions of public sector workers and brings them continuous fear for their livelihood. Also it further increases the enormous differences between the rich, who can afford private education, private health care etc., and the poor who cannot.

This book is extremely welcome and timely. It brings together an enormous amount of detail from very different sections of the public sector on what privatisation means and how it is introduced. The book shows that there is a clear and connected campaign for privatising public services in which the political interests of Thatcherite Tories are joined by the economic interests of large concerns in catering, cleaning, health care and management consultancy. This book also makes clear that the Government can be deflected from pursuing its aims as in the case of the attempted privatisation of the Gas Showrooms. This example showed clearly how broad support — by workers, consumers and sections of the supplying industries — for keeping the showrooms in public ownership has been effective in shifting the Government.

This book will be of practical value to workers and trade union represenatatives fighting to keep valuable services public. It should also provoke considerable discussion in the labour movement. The history of Thatcherism has shown that the basic principles on which the labour movement has rested, such as public ownership or the welfare state, are accepted but not actively supported by sufficient people, leaving them vulnerable to the onslaught of backward-looking conservatives.

This realisation is forcing upon the labour movement the urgency of once again making public services truly popular. For too long unions have allowed the enemies of state intervention to vilify public services as inefficient, monopolistic and a burden on the "productive" resources of the nation. We need to mount an effective campaign in support of our services which seeks to demonstrate how public services could be improved with the introduction of greater workers' and users' control of the services. At the present time many public services are organised in such a way as to mirror the private sector. The managerial cost cutting mentality is in the public services as it is in private industry. We all formally "own" the public services through the agencies of central and local government, but for workers and users of those services the feeling of powerlessness can be just as strong as it can when we speak of the conditions in the private sector. This should not be the case. As socialists we believe that public enterprise is superior in all ways to private industry and we need to win peoples' minds for its ideals. We need to show in practice that this is the case.

The most effective way that this can be achieved is by opening up the services to democratic control by workers and users. In the labour movement we are only just beginning to think about how this can be done. We must think fast because if we are not capable of building broad popular support for public services and for state intervention in general, it is likely that we will witness the obliteration of social progress achieved by the labour movement. This book helps us to begin to discuss some of these questions and it is therefore to be welcomed.

I hope that many people who work in the public sector and many people who rely on public services will read this book. I hope they will realise once more the importance of the public services and ask themselves what they can do to defend them against privatisation.

Rodney K. Bickerstaffe
General Secretary, NUPE

Introduction
Privatisation—is it really an issue?

Sue Hastings & Hugo Levie
(TURU)

How this book came about

This book grew out of a seminar, on union responses to privatisation, organised by the Trade Union Research Unit, and held at Ruskin College, Oxford, on the 21st July 1982.

Only a few days before the seminar, Sir Geoffrey Howe had made a speech in Cambridge glorying in the privatisation which had already taken place, and suggesting new ways in which the public sector might be invaded by private sector organisations. Only two days before the seminar, the Government had issued its white paper on the privatisation of British Telecom. So those at the seminar were well aware that they were not contributing to a post mortem on privatisation, but were comparing the responses of their unions to an ongoing and growing crisis.

The word 'grew', in the first sentence of this introduction, was used advisedly. Six papers were presented to the seminar, with a preliminary survey provided by TURU. Several of the papers have been extended before inclusion in the book, and in most cases an indication of the issues raised in discussion has been added. An extra contribution, on privatisation in the health service, has been supplied by COHSE, to fill one obvious gap in the original contributions.

What is, and is not, included?

The book does not cover every single act of privatisation which has occurred since 1979. It does not, for instance, have a separate section on the British National Oil Corporation whose privatisation was extremely important politically, but of less significance in terms of the union response. The introductory survey does, however, deal superficially with very many aspects of privatisation in order to illustrate the impact it has made on every sector of the economy.

The main part of the book consists of contributions from seven of the unions which have already had to make a positive response to privatisation proposals.

The first is a graphic description by a Wandsworth NUPE shop steward and a full-time union officer of what it is like to be privatised.

The COHSE paper reasserts, what is in danger of being forgotten, that the NHS must be defended because, despite its deficiencies, it provides medical care for people according to their need rather than their ability to pay for its services.

The NALGO contribution compares two specific areas, gas and electricity showrooms, where privatisation proposals have been made but not yet implemented. An important conclusion is that cross-subsidisation of services, while perfectly acceptable in private sector companies, may be regarded as 'unfair competition' in the public sector.

The privatisation of the National Freight Corporation is analysed in detail in the TGWU contribution. The TGWU opposed the management buy-out of the NFC, but other unions involved did not. The privatisation of the company will be a severe hindrance to an integrated transport policy under a future Labour Government.

The POEU paper on British Telecom deals mainly with the effects of liberalisation and privatisation on domestic consumers. By increasing installation charges to an 'economic' level above the price which those without telephones can afford, BT is in danger of reducing demand for its own services.

The construction industry is already largely privately owned, so it provides an opportunity for comparing working conditions in the public and private sections. Not surprisingly, as the UCATT paper shows, conditions are worse in the latter; the surprise is how much worse.

The interesting point about the contribution on privatisation in the Civil Service from SCPS is that the aim of 'hiving off' hunks of the Civil Service is seen as reducing numbers of civil servants and hence the physical size of the public sector rather than simply saving money.

The last contribution describes the strategies adopted by NUPE and Services to Community Action and Tenants (SCAT) to combat the contracting out of local authority services. Education and propaganda are key elements in the strategy, and NUPE has produced effective material to back up the policy. Many of the photos in the book come from their campaign packs.

It is very clear from all the papers that, while the employees of public sector organisations are the first to be affected by privatisation, in the longer term the consumers will also suffer. The contributions share a common point of view, but the contents of each remain the responsibility of the contributor or contributing research department.

Because privatisation continues apace, relevant events have occurred since the seminar in many of the areas covered by the papers. They have been exluded, on the grounds that a line must be drawn somewhere. The issues raised remain much the same.

The seminar in Oxford was one of a series on the issues currently facing unions; the previous one had been on fighting redundancies.* The aim of the series is to set the particular problems confronting union officials in the context of the similar difficulties experienced by other unions.

Union responses to privatisation

Any particular act of privatisation is part of a much wider Tory Campaign to totally dismantle the public sector. The campaign has been opposed on general grounds by the TUC; and in specific instances by the relevant unions, and in some cases by the boards of the corporations and their consumers. Sometimes opposition to privatisation has led to delay, or to changes in the proposals, but the inexorable march goes on.

Unions make different responses to privatisation, as the papers show. They still need to consider how they can best support each other both at head office and at grass roots level; what exchanges of information and tactics can usefully be made.

The main part of a union response to privatisation often involves reacting to proposed redundancies and/or changes in working conditions. Where these considerations are paramount, acceptance of some form of private control may be regarded as preferable to outright opposition and serious job losses. Building on board or consumer opposition may be a feasible policy for unions to pursue. It may be necessary to consider alternative union proposals or even tendering for a contract.

In the longer term unions will have to consider whether and how

---

* The extended report of this seminar is to be published in book form by Spokesman later in 1983.

privatisation could be reversed; and how worker participation and control in the public sector could be improved.

The discussion in this book does not answer these questions, but it provides a starting point for future consideration.

Who or what is 'privatisation'?

The word, 'privatisation', is often heard these days, but it is not to be found in the Oxford English Dictionary, nor in most other English dictionaries. It does, however, occur, as a verb, in Webster's Third New International Dictionary (1961 edition) where it is defined in the following way:

'privatize(sic) — to alter the status of (as a business or industry) from public to private control or ownership'.

This sounds very much like denationalisation and in fact the two terms are often used synonymously. For instance, a Tory Minister earlier this year indicated that 'privatisation' meant "the transfer of ownership from the state to private enterprise of as many public sector businesses as possible".*

But the scope of the word is frequently extended to include the use of private contractors to provide services previously provided by public sector employees. And in a Cambridge lecture at the beginning of July this year, Sir Geoffrey Howe included among his suggestions for further loosening "the grip of the public sector": faster growth of private health insurance, increased use of charges for social services, student loans, and more "community involvement in the financing and management of local schools".** (All this in the name of 'more consumer choice'!!)

So, in practice, privatisation covers a multitude of sins, including:

a. Selling off nationalised concerns, either to their management and/or workforce (National Freight Company); or to private shareholders (as is proposed for British Airways). A legal reconstruction of the public corporation as a public company is usually required before such a sale can take place.

b. Public issue of a minority or a majority of shares on the Stock Exchange (e.g. British Aerospace, Cable and Wireless, and as

---

* Mr Nicholas Ridley, Finance Secretary to the Treasury, 12 February 1982.
** For a detailed report of the speech, see *Financial Times,* 5th July 1982.

Privatisation is new, but attacks on the public sector are not — a demonstration against cuts in the NHS in April 1976.

proposed for the British National Oil Corporation). Again the concern must have previously been converted into a public company.

c. Placement of shares with institutional investors (as with the Government's minority shareholding in the British Sugar Corporation).

d. Sales of physical assets (such as British Rail's hotels, and New Town industrial and commercial properties).

e. Joint public/private sector ventures (such as the setting up of Allied Steel and Wire, an independent company in the private sector formed by the British Steel Corporation and GKN; and the merger of British Rail's hovercraft service with Hoverlloyd).

f. Allowing private competition where a public corporation previously had monopoly rights (as was done under the 1980 Transport Act for express coach routes and under the 1981 British Telecommunications Act for British Telecom).

g. Making it possible, and encouraging, private contractors to tender to provide services previously provided within the public sector (such as catering and laundry services in the NHS, refuse collections for some local authorities).

h. Setting up a scheme to introduce private finance into large scale construction projects (as with the proposals for private funding for road building drawn up by the Civil Engineering Economic Development Council — EDC).

The main *motives for privatisation* are usually given as*:

a. The improved and more efficient use of public sector resources by 'opening up new areas to market forces, wherever this can be done' and by 'returning industries and activities to the private sector'.

b. 'Wider share ownership' through sales of shares in public sector enterprises to individual investors and pension funds; and through the extension of share ownership among employees under preferential arrangements or under some form of buy-out, as in the case of the National Freight Company.

c. A reduction of 'the burden on the Exchequer' of the public sector via receipts from sales of assets, and via 'the removal from the public sector borrowing requirement (PSBR) of any future borrowing by the bodies concerned'.

The last of these has acquired increasing significance with the failure of the Government's monetary policies and the need to reduce PSBR sharply.

There are clear replies to each of the arguments set out above:

a. More efficient running of nationalised concerns is perfectly possible within the public sector, where the requirements of employees and consumers are more likely to receive attention. In many areas of the public sector, moreover, the social benefits of providing services are more important than economic efficiency.

b. 'Wider share ownership' is a misleading phrase because it says nothing about *control* of the companies concerned. Employee share owners usually have very little say in the running of their company.

c. There is no reason why public sector bodies should not obtain investment funds from sources other than the treasury while still remaining in the public sector. The Treasury argument against this point of view is that the taxpayer then becomes financially responsible for the public corporations (as if he/she were not already) and that the ban is a form of financial restraint. For

* See, for example, Treasury Economic Progress Report, No.145, May 1982, pp.1-2 — from which the phrases in inverted commas are taken.

what it is worth the Treasury case on borrowing by nationalised industries from the private capital market is:

> All we say is that there has to be a restraint and a limit at some point, and the reason for that is that these industries are owned by the Government and are public statutory corporations which cannot go bust. Whether we issue a formal guarantee or not, they borrow in the Government's name, the Government's credit is engaged, and the taxpayer stands behind it. To supplement that, they also, in many cases, have a degree of monopoly power. So they have an enormous borrowing power, almost to commandeer funds. This means that one has to make some judgment about what total they should spend. You may take the view that we have arrived at the wrong total, but I do not think one should dispute that there should be a limit put on somewhere.*

The real *arguments against denationalisation,* which equally apply to the other forms of privatisation, were clearly stated in a TUC paper in December, 1981**:

i. the Government is penalising successful public enterprise, because the private sector will buy only profitable assets;

ii. far from denationalisation helping the funding of public expenditure, as the Government argues, the Exchequer loses income from the profitable nationalised industries and is left with the funding of the unprofitable industries;

iii. denationalisation is unnecessarily disruptive when most industries are in recession;

iv. denationalisation and liberalisation are likely to break up an industry's network of services, and therefore hit the ability of a nationalised industry to cross-subsidise; and

v. liberalisation leads to "cream-skimming", as private companies in such industries as the bus, aviation and telecommunications industries introduce new services only in the profitable sectors.

What has happened in reality during the period 1979 to 1982 is described in detail in the following sections. What emerges is a picture of continuing struggle for workers in the public sector and a picture of increasing hardship for those dependent on the public services.

---

* Treasury and Civil Service Committee, Report on the Financing of the Nationalised Industries, 1980-1, HC 348-11, Q.153.
** TUC Background Paper B, Nationalised Industries Conference, December 1981, p.6.

1. Privatisation: 1979-82

Sue Hastings
(TURU Research Associate)

Privatisation policy — a diary

1979 *The Tory Manifesto* — no mention of 'privatisation' but the section on nationalisation contained proposals for:

a. selling back to private ownership the then recently nationalised aerospace and shipbuilding industries, with opportunities for employees to purchase shares;

b. selling shares in the National Freight Company to the public to get private investment;

c. relaxing the system of licensing by Traffic Commissioners to enable new bus services to be set up, and encouraging new private operators;

d. amending the 1975 Industry Act to restrict the powers of the National Enterprise Board and to force it to sell assets;

e. less interference and clearer financial discipline for those industries which remained nationalised.

So, many of the ingredients of privatisation were already collected together in one section of the Manifesto; and other sections included plans to review the British National Oil Corporation, and to sell off council houses to their tenants.

1979 June: *Howe's First Budget* — Howe did not refer to privatisation and the only specific proposal he made was for the sale of National Enterprise Board (NEB) assets. He spoke in general terms of 'making savings in public spending and rolling back the boundaries of the public sector' and also said:

> "Sales of state-owned assets to the private sector serve the immediate purpose of helping to reduce the excessive public

sector borrowing requirement with which I was faced.

But such sales . . . are (also) an essential part of our long-term programme for promoting the widest possible participation by people in the ownership of British industry. This objective — wider public ownership in the true meaning of the term — has implications not merely for the scale of our programme, but also for the methods of sale we shall adopt".*

1980 In spite of these general platitudes, several Acts were passed in the first Session of Parliament under the Tories, which in fact paved the way for ensuing acts of privatisation.

Each Bill was argued in Parliament as being advantageous to the individual industry. For instance, Sir Keith Joseph said in the Second Reading Debate on the British Aerospace Bill:

"We do not believe that nationalisation is the right framework for so intensely competitive and sophisticated an industry".*

And the Minister piloting the Civil Aviation Bill through Parliament argued that British Airways should be a 'normal private sector company', although, in fact, only a minority of the newly constituted company's shares were to be offered — first to British Airways employees, and then to pensions funds.**

In retrospect, it is obvious that the legislation of 1980 was the vanguard of a concerted campaign to reduce the public sector to its bare bones.

1981 Two further major pieces of privatisation legislation were pushed through Parliament: the 1981 *Transport Act* which enabled British Rail to be told to sell off its subsidiaries, and which set up a holding company to control the reconstituted British Transport Docks Board; and the *British Telecommunications Act* (discussed below).

1981 December. The Hundred Group of Chartered Accountants issued *The Financing of State-owned Industries,* which aroused considerable interest and which put forward new proposals for financing the nationalised industries. These included access to private sector finance for public corporations at the discretion of their managements, and exclusion of borrowing not made through government channels from the Public Sector Borrowing Requirement (PSBR).

* HC Debate, vol. 974, c.213.
** HC Debate, vol.974, c.36-9.

Privatisation — the sums
— from the Treasury Economic Progress Report, May 1982

SPECIAL SALES OF ASSETS
(effects on public expenditure)

1979-80 £m cash

Net reductions in expenditure

Sales of shares in the British Petroleum Co Ltd (BP)	276
National Enterprise Board — sale of certain shares	37
Sale of shares in Drake & Scull Holdings Ltd	1
New Town Development Corps and the Commission for the New Towns — sale of land and Buildings	26
Regional Water Authorities — sale of land	3
Sale of shares in Suez Finance Co	22
Property Services Agency — sale of land and buildings	5
TOTAL	370

Revenue offsets to planned expenditure

British National Oil Corp — receipts of advanced payments for oil	622
Stamp duty and VAT	7
GRAND TOTAL	999

Net reductions in expenditure

Receipt of premiums levied on the seventh round of North Sea oil licences (less £15m of payments on licences granted to British National Oil Corp)	195
Sale of leases of certain motorway service areas — sales of land and buildings	28
Property Services Agency — sale of land and buildings	4
Sale of shares in British Aerospace Ltd	43
New Town Development Corps and the Commission for New Towns — sale of land and buildings	52
National Enterprise Board — sales of certain shares	83
TOTAL	405

Revenue offsets to planned expenditure

Change in level of receipts of advance payments for oil	−49
GRAND TOTAL	356

1981-82
Net reductions in expenditure

Motorway service area leases	19
British Sugar Corporation	44
Cable and Wireless	182
New Towns	73
Oil stockpile	50
Sale of other stocks	19
Amersham International	64
Forestry Commission	7
National Freight Company	5
NEB subsidaries	2
Crown Agents — sale of property	7
Property Service Agency properties	1

Government's nil-paid rights in 1982

BP rights issue	8
TOTAL	481

Revenue offsets to planned expenditure

British National Oil Corporation — effect of delivery in 1981-82 of oil for which advance payment was received in 1980-81	−573
GRAND TOTAL	−92

Privatisation — The legislation, 1980

Acts passed which incorporated enabling provisions* allowing privatisation to take place were:

1. Industry Act, 1980 (cap.33) — Sections 1-7 altered the status and financing of the NEB.

2. Housing Act, 1980 (cap.51) established a statutory 'right to buy' for tenants of houses and flats owned by local authorities.

3. Local Government Planning & Land Act, 1980 (cap.65) — work on highway & housing maintenance to be offered to competitive tender to the private sector.

4. British Aerospace Act, 1980 (cap.26) — sole purpose of Act to rest all property, rights, etc of British Aerospace in a company nominated by the Secretary of State.

5. Civil Aviation Act, 1980 (cap.60) — reduction of public dividend capital of British Airways Board; dissolution of BAB and subsequent vesting of property etc in a public company.

6. Transport Act 1980 (cap.34) — relaxation of traffic licensing on road passenger transport; conversion of National Freight Corporation into a public company.

*The privatisation measures of each of these Acts were argued for by Ministers on the grounds that nationalisation was unsuitable for that particular industry.

1982 January. An alternative suggestion was put forward in a paper published by the Institute of Directors.* This was that the Government guarantee on borrowing by the nationalised industries should be reduced. For instance, the Government might guarantee £100 stock only up to £70, with the non-guaranteed portion being excluded from the PSBR.

1982 In spite of the discussion about alternative means of financing, more privatisation legislation went through Parliament. The *Oil and Gas (Enterprise) Bill* affected both the British National Oil Corporation and the British Gas Corporation. The *Transport Bill* reconstituted the National Bus Company as a public company, and allowed the Government to sell off the Heavy Goods Vehicle testing stations.

* J.B. Bracewell-Milnes: Privatisation of Nationalised Industries — Private Financing through Partially Guaranteed Securities.

1982 March. The TUC launched its campaign to resist further moves towards the use of private contractors by local authorities.

1982 July. In a speech widely regarded as anticipating Tory party discussion on their next Election Manifesto, Sir Geoffrey Howe talked of further privatisation of the public utilities and corporations, a transfer of local authority functions to private enterprise, and of privatisation of aspects of health and education.

The next target — education? A day nursery in Hackney

Privatisation — Step by Step

This section shows how different forms of privatisation have spread into all areas of the public sector; and how the trickle of 'privatisation' measures of the first year of Tory Government is rapidly turning into a flood.

Transport*

● **Road Passenger Transport.** The 1980 Transport Act (s.5), by relaxing the traffic licensing system, from 6th October 1980, has encouraged the development of express coach services, both by National Bus Company subsidiaries and by private operators, often in competition with British Rail train services. The Treasury claim 'that there has been a rapid development of express coach services and reductions in fares on many routes'.** There has also been cut-throat competition which both private and public sector operators have found difficult to sustain. In 1981, NBC carried 50 per cent more express coach passengers than in the previous year, but 8.5 per cent less stage coach passengers, with a reduction of 8 per cent in mileage (mainly stage coach) covered.*** The following article illustrates the issues:

Cut-price coaches boost travel Financial Times, *18.10.80.*
The new era of cut-price long distance coach travel, ushered in by the removal of virtually all licensing restrictions nearly two weeks ago, appears to have brought a big increase in passengers.

British Coachways, the private enterprise consortium set up to take on the state-owned National Express, says that results have exceeded expectations. The nationalised former monopoly holder, which cut fares in response, say business is noticeably higher than a year ago and British Rail "hasn't noticed" any downturn in traffic on the routes involved.

The substantial fares cut introduced by British Coachways and partially countered by National Express's stand-buy fares may have generated a new market, National Express said yesterday. "With a £2 fare from London to Birmingham it is now arguably cheaper than hitch-hiking", said National Express.

Mr Michael Kay, marketing manager of British Coachways, said yesterday that the consortium would be carrying 2,000 passengers this weekend and that it expected to carry its 10,000th passenger by the end of this month. Three new members have joined the original six operators in the group, including Bartons of Nottingham with about 300 coaches, bringing BC's coach pool to more than 1,000 units.

Mr Kay said that traffic on all eight routes from London had been high, in every case exceeding the 80 per cent load factor which the coaches needed to be profitable. The Birmingham service had been

---

* See also TGWU paper on the NFC, p.109.
** Treasury Economic Progress Report, May 1982, p.3.
*** National Bus Company, Annual Report 1981, see *Financial Times,* 17th June 1982.

very successful and so also had the Glasgow service (with a single fare of £7.50) with nine coach-loads coming down at the weekends. On the Plymouth and Bristol routes a daily service had had to be introduced instead of three a week as planned.

From the beginning of next month BC will introduce four new services from London — to Bournmouth, Edinburgh, Dundee and Perth — and also a Swansea-Birmingham service.

In fact our target of carrying 600,000 passengers by the start of the tourest season next May, which I had regarded as rather pie in the sky, now seems possible", said Mr Kay.

The consortium has had some problems, partly caused by the fast public reaction and partly by National Express banning BC coaches from its bus stations in Exeter, Sheffield and Cardiff. This has forced BC to make arrangements with local police authorities for temporary pick-up and set-down points but the group is having discussions with the local authorities who lease the coach station grounds to National Express.

"All our members are well established coach operators and we hope some local authorities may be persuaded to lean slightly on National Express", Mr Kay said.

The consortium has advertised its facilities widely in local newspapers in the areas involved and is making full use of travel agents' facilities, offering them up to 13 per cent commission in London and 10 per cent in the provinces.

National Express said yesterday that it was "very pleased" with the amount of business it had received since its routes were opened to competition. "We believe there has been a general increase as a result of the amount of publicity that has been generated".

Traffic was higher than at this time a year ago, particularly on the trunk routes with competing services. "We believe the lower fares have opened a new market, attracting people outside the coach trade", National Express said.

British Rail is countering with its "go anywhere for £1" offer during November for senior citizens with Railcards and has cut the price of its Family Railcard from £16 to £5.

If competition continues to increase on the main trunk routes, however, with National Express having to operate with lower profit margins, one casualty may be its network of less profitable rural services.

One of the dilemmas of privatisation for employees and consumers was illustrated by the Transport Minister's decision in March 1980 to allow a workers' private bus service at Cradley Heath, West Midlands against the wishes of the local authority bus group*.

The 1982 Transport Bill permits the introduction of private

* *Financial Times,* 1 April 1980.

capital into the National Bus Company, specifically into its National Express (which runs express coach services) and National Holidays subsidiaries, and into its property holdings (mainly bus and coach stations). Together these operating subsidiaries made a contribution of £4.5m working profit towards NBC's total operating profit of £25.3m in 1981.

The hiving off of National Express and National Holidays is opposed by the NBC Board on the grounds that it would lose its flexibility and therefore not be able to run the core business in a viable manner.

However, the Board is not opposed to the introduction of private capital into the property portfolio as this could lead to improvements in these facilities.*

● **Roads.** The administration of road construction work was hived off to 'private consultants' following a review of the Departmental role in 1979. The Comptroller and Auditor General claims that the change cost up to £10m in 1981-82:

Change to private firms to cost taxpayer £10m Times *14.1.82*
A ministerial decision to hive off the administration of road construction work to private consultants will cost the taxpayer up to £10m in the current financial year.

The hidden cost of the de-nationalisation move, with continuing losses in future years, has been revealed in a report written by Mr Gordon Downey, the Comptroller and Auditor General. He says that responsibility for £2,000m of road contracts, organised by the Ministry of Transport, has been transferred to 15 consultant engineering firms "despite the extra costs involved".

The report, which will be considered by the Commons Committee of Public Accounts, shows than an estimated £4m will be paid out in redundancy money to about 1,700 staff. Mr Downey tells MPs: "Since many of the staff had been re-employed by consulting engineers, on similar duties and often in the same location, I asked the department what steps they have taken to reduce the incidence of redundancy payments in such cases.

"They pointed out that employees were statutorily entitled to redundancy payments, even where their existing employer found a new employer for them."

The Comptroller also reports that the Ministry has agreed to pay the private consultants a familiarisation fee of up to £1,250,000 to compensate them for taking on design work completed by the old sub-units.

But the most important portion of this year's £10m loss is

* NBC Annual Report 1981; *Financial Times,* 17 June 1982.

explained by a Whitehall study which concluded "that although there was no significant difference in the efficiency of performance, it costs more to employ consulting engineers than viable sub-units".

On the Ministry's own figures, the extra costs could be as high as £4.7m in the current year, with a similar "penalty" next year, which would "probably" diminish in future years. A review of the work of the sub-units was launched in 1979 because cutbacks in the road building programmes undoubtedly made the sub-units less efficient.

NEDO's civil engineering EDC drew up plans to introduce private finance into road construction. The Environment and Transport Ministers, Heseltine and Howell, approved the proposal in principle in April 1982. Various schemes, and methods of apportioning risk, were discussed and the views of the Federation of Civil Engineering Constractors sought. It was thought that a test scheme for private sector financing might start early in 1983.*

However, the Federation of Civil Engineering Contractors have rejected the Transport Department's proposals. The Federation's objections are that the scheme is unworkable and places an unacceptable burden of risk on contractors. 'The principle of raising private funds as an additional source of finance for road building programmes is, however, supported by the Federation.'**

Motorway service areas have been sold. The 1982 Transport Bill includes provision for the powers for the testing of heavy goods vehicles (HGV) to be transferred to the private sector. The Institute of Professional Civil Servants (IPCS) has proposed setting up a non-profit making company to buy the HGV testing stations and hold them until they can be returned to the public sector. Their aim is to safeguard the jobs of employees including 450 professional engineering IPCS members.***

● **Air Transport.** The Civil Aviation Act, 1980 provided for a reduction of the public dividend capital of the *British Airways Board,* for the Board's dissolution, and for the subsequent vesting of its property, rights, etc., in a company nominated by the Secretary of State.

In his speech on the Second Reading of the Bill the Minister

---

* *Financial Times,* 29th April 1982, Ministers back private funds for roads; 16th June 1982, Private funding for roads may start next year.
** *Financial Times,* 17 July 1982: Finance scheme for roads rejected.
*** See *Times,* 18th May 1982: Union plans to go into business to save jobs.

argued that British Airways should be a 'normal private sector company'. He later said that only a minority of shares would be sold initially and that they would first be offered to employees of British Airways, and then to pension funds and other institutions.

"We shall be providing for public ownership in the true and proper meaning of the term"*

However, the plan to sell shares in British Airways came unstuck when BA made substantial post-tax losses of £145m in 1980-81, and probably more than £200m in 1981-82. The workforce was reduced by 9,000 to cut costs and on 30th April, 1982 it was announced in a written answer to a Parliamentary Question that Britain Airways would be split into three separate divisions, or 'profit centres' — International Services, European Services and Gatwick Services.

"These steps have been taken in order to make British Airways more efficient, more sensitive to the· wishes of travellers, and more profitable with a view to placing it in the private sector as soon as possible."**

British Airways has delayed publishing its annual report and accounts, possibly so that the full costs of the year's redundancies can be included. It has been suggested that there may be further cuts in 'unprofitable routes'.

British Airways confirmed in July that it intends reducing its workforce by a further 7,000 by March 1983 (on top of 9,000 jobs lost in the last year, 23,000 over the last three years). The redundancies are said to be necessary to bring BA to profitability before privatisation, presently planned for late 1983. Mr Iain Sproat, Aviation Minister, says BA is undergoing an almost 'miraculous transformation'(!)***

And, although it has never been on any list of public corporations to be privatised, it was suggested in a recent article in the *The Times*† that Mr Sproat, Minister of State at the Department of Trade, is keen to introduce private capital into the *British Airports Authority*. The article goes on to say that as

---

* HC Debate, vol.974, c.36-9.
** HC Debate, 30.4.82, c.356w.
*** *Guardian,* 12th July 1982, British Airways will cut 7,000 more jobs.
† *Times,* 23rd June 1982. p.15.

the BAA derives most of its income from monopoly landing charges, a sale of shares would not be easy to implement. The idea of a bond, a non-redeemable preference share guaranteeing the holder a proportion of the authority's profits, is apparently being canvassed instead.

A report from the Centre for Policy Studies has been published suggesting that the *British Airports Authority* should be broken up and private companies allowed to run individual airports.* The BAA prefers its own proposals for the injection of private capital.

The Royal Aircraft Establishment's airfield at Farnborough has been the subject of a Ministry of Defence study. The option of closing it down has been rejected, but some part of it may be leased to business aviation operators.**

● **Docks.** The 1981 Transport Act (c.56) established a holding company to control the reconstituted British Transport Docks Board, to be known as Associated British Ports. The Government hope to sell 49 per cent of the equity in 1982-83 and have declared that they will not take an active role in its affairs after that.

● **Railways.** Even British Rail, unlikely ever to be a candidate for outright sale to the private sector, has not been immune from the privatisation trend.

A subsidiary company, *British Rail Investments Ltd.,* (BRIL), was set up to handle the introduction of private capital into some operations. Several hotels, and some other property assets, have already been sold. The hovercraft subsidiary has merged with Hoverlloyd, its main competitor, to form a new company, Hoverspeed. And BRIL is drawing up proposals for the introduction of private capital into Sealink (UK) Ltd. Because most of the businesses to be sold are relatively small and not necessarily related to a railway business, legislation was not needed for most of these changes. There were, however, some legal points on ports to be resolved and these were cleared up in the 1981 Transport Act.

● **Transport privatisation — a comment.** The very far-reaching privatisation in the areas of transport described above

---

* Financial Times, 13.7.82: Airports UK — A policy for the UK's Civil Airports.
** *Financial Times,* 14.7.82 MoD may lease off part of Farnborough to business.

constitutes an attempt to convert *services* into *businesses*, more or less efficient. There is a very obvious danger that the effect will be the loss of transport services in areas where they cannot be run profitably (rural bus services, small ports, for example) and a lack of consideration of the needs of consumers and employees.

Energy

● **North Sea Oil.** The 1979 Tory manifesto pledged that there would be a complete review of the operations of the *British National Oil Corporation* (BNOC). This review took some time and it was not until December 1981 that the Oil and Gas (Enterprise) Bill was introduced in the House of Commons. The Bill became an Act in June 1982.

Under the Act, the oil exploitation and production businesses of BNOC are to be converted into a limited liability company called Britoil. The Government propose selling 51 per cent of the new company's shares to the public and do not intend to use their rights as shareholders to intervene in commercial decisions. They do intend, however, to retain special rights in the Articles of Association of the company 'to prevent any unacceptable change in its future control'.* The trading part of BNOC's activities is to be retained in the public sector, and will probably increase its staffing from 60 to about 100 to enable it to operate independently.

The actual organisation of the Corporation's structure, with a transfer of the 2,350 staff, took place in November 1982 with the sale of Britoil shares. On the basis of current oil prices and of prospects for the near future, it has been estimated that the sale of shares could raise between £600m and £750m for the Treasury. It has been suggested by commentators that the Government could opt for a phased sale, giving investors the opportunity to pay for part of their purchases next year.**

● **Gas.** The Oil and Gas (Enterprise) Act does *not* provide for the introduction of private capital into the British Gas Corporation. In fact, the BGC stated that it thought this would be a preferable form of privatisation to 'the piecemeal back-up of an economic

---

* Treasury Economic Progress Report, May 1982, p.4
** *Financial Times,* 24th June 1982: *Guardian,* 29th June 1982.

structure which has a proven record of success.*

The Act provides several methods for privatising parts of BGC. It enables BGC assets to be disposed of and the Government have made clear that they intend to dispose first of the Corporation's oil-producing interests in the North Sea. At the demand, under existing legislation, of Nigel Lawson, the Energy Secretary, the Corporation's 50 per cent holding in the *Wytch Farm oil field* in Dorset is already in the process of being sold off.

The new Act would also enable the Government to require the BGC to dispose of the gas showrooms — a proposal deriving from the Monopolies and Mergers Commission report on the Gas Corporation published in 1980. The Government have, however, committed themselves to introducing regulations, for example, on the training of private sector gas-fitters, to ensure that safety standards are not reduced, and this cannot be done before the next session of Parliament. So the Energy Secretary gave the Corporation's board and unions, both of whom strongly oppose the compulsory sale of the showrooms, a year to devise its own method of disposal, that is until the end of 1982.**

BGC's monopoly position in buying gas, and in supplying it to large industrial and commercial consumers, is removed by the Oil and Gas (Enterprise) Act. A potential private supplier would apparently have to negotiate access to the grid with the Corporation, but could appeal to the Energy Secretary if unsuccessful. The Government hopes that the arrangements will encourage more exploration for gas.

The BGC is left with a monopoly in the supply of gas only to smaller consumers whom they have a statutory obligation to supply on request — mainly domestic consumers. Higher prices to these consumers appear inevitable.

Even in this area, Nigel Lawson is seeking to improve "efficiency". He told the annual conference of the International Association of Energy Economists in Cambridge in June 1982:

> "Where we can neither privatise nor introduce real competition we have to do our best to stimulate market disciplines."

* BGC Statement following the proposals for the Gas Corporation announced in the Queen's Speech in November 1981. Sir Denis Rooke, the Corporation's Chairman was 'carpeted' by Nigel Lawson on account of the statement.

** See *Financial Times*, 10th November 1981, British Gas given year to devise showroom plan. See also the NALGO paper on showrooms, p.92.

He cited external financing as one means of doing this, but said that the Government was reinforcing these controls by setting clearer objectives and performance targets for public corporations — and that British Gas had been ordered to *reduce its operating costs* by 5 per cent by April 1983. Further, management consultants were being brought in to carry out an efficiency examination of the BGC.*

In fact, BGC have appointed their own controller of efficiency studies to combat criticism and help it meet government efficiency targets. Nevertheless, the effect of the gas levy and of reduced demand has been a fall in profits of 20 per cent in 1981-82.**

● **Electricity.** In the speech in Cambridge mentioned above, Mr Lawson said that the Government was planning 'shortly' to introduce legislation to encourage the *supply of electricity by the private sector* by allowing it to carry out this activity as a main business, rather than as a subsidiary business as is allowed at present.

The CEGB has been the subject of a recent Monopolies and Mergers Commission investigation.

● **Coal.** The NCB is also the subject of a Monopolies and Mergers Commission Inquiry.

The NCB, in consultation with the Treasury, is reported*** to be trying to hive off to private investors some of its coal stocks to reduce stock financing costs, currently over £120m per year. The plan involves establishing a futures market for coal, with banks lending money to finance agreed amounts of stock, and the loans being repaid with the coal as sold in accordance with the agreement.

● **Energy privatisation. A comment.** As with transport, privatisation is seen to be extending into all corners of the energy sector. The dispute over the gas showrooms, although much publicised, turns out to be only one facet of an onslaught on the energy monopolies. The effects are almost certain to include higher prices to consumers and fewer jobs for employees.

---

* See *Financial Times,* 29th June 1982, British Gas told to cut operating costs by 5 per cent.
** *Financial Times,* 13th July 1982 and 19th July 1982.
*** *Financial Times,* 5th July 1982, NCB may hive off stocks to private investors.

Communications*

- **British Telecom.** *British Telecom* (BT) was established as a separate public corporation from October 1981 under the British Telecommunications Act 1981. The Act allowed BT to operate through subsidiaries or in partnership with private firms. It also gave the Government power to require BT to transfer activities to wholly-owned subsidiaries and then to dispose of them.

  However, on 20th July 1982 the Minister made a widely expected announcement on the conversion of the whole of BT into a public limited company (Cmnd. 8610):

  > "as the first step towards the eventual sale of shares in the organisation to private investors."**

  This will require legislation, probably next session, including provision for a regulatory body for telecommunications. There may not be time for sale of BT assets before the end of this Parliament, but, with net assets of £8bn, BT's sale would be the largest act of privatisation so far.

  On the same day the Centre for Policy Studies published a paper supporting privatisation in telecommunications.

- **Cable and Wireless.** The 1981 Act allowed the Government to dispose of its shares in *Cable and Wireless*. Nearly half its shares were sold in the autumn of 1981.

  Cable and Wireless made profits of £97.7m in the year ending 31st March 1982, higher than expected when the Government sold half its shares last autumn — so the gain goes to private investors.

- **Mercury.** Under the 1981 Act the Secretary of State for Industry can license companies other than BT to run telecommunications systems. In February 1982 he announced that he had granted a 25-year license to *Mercury* to run an independent system in competition with BT. Mercury is financed 40 per cent by Cable and Wireless, 40 per cent by BP (familiar names?!) and 20 per cent by Barclays Merchant Bank. It was strongly urged to get together by the Department of Industry. At the beginning of July 1982, Sir Michael Edwardes became a non-executive director of Mercury with the prospect of becoming Chairman

---

* See also POEU Research Department paper on p.130.
** *Financial Times,* 5th July 1982 Privatisation plan for Telecom likely this month.

when his term at BL ends at the end of 1982. Mercury is behind with its plans to develop a network covering major business centres, using optical fibres laid alongside British Rail track, but the first inter-city link is expected in autumn 1983.

Other network services which compete with BT's, but using the BT network, have also been licensed, including mail box, and store and forward facilities.

On the 25th June 1982 Patrick Jenkin, in a written reply to a Parliamentary Question (to secure minimum publicity) told the House of Commons that he was inviting BT and the private sector to submit competitive proposals for new radio-telephone networks.

● **Apparatus.** By giving the Secretary of State powers to approve standards of apparatus attached to the BT network, the 1981 Act enabled him to open up the supply of apparatus to free competition. In order to keep pace with the anticipated competition BT have been forced into making available for sale most of the types of the telephone which are usually rented.*

However, it appears that the large-scale use of unsuitable privately supplied equipment could cause fundamental damage to the BT network. So regulations prohibiting the use of non-approved equipment have had to be introduced with prosecution for those who do not comply.** (Is private competition worth all this?).

● **Private finance.** In his 1982 Budget, Sir Geoffrey Howe announced approval in principle for the issue by BT of a bond to raise capital from the market, the *Buzby Bond*. He said it would be 'an important experiment in exposing the performance of a nationalised industry to the judgment of the market place. It is hoped to launch the bond in autumn 1982, but that depends on market conditions at the time.

At its annual conference the Post Office Engineering Union passed a resolution commiting the union to stop privatisation. And the British Telecom Union Committee has asked the TUC for full support in its campaign against privatisation. It argues that Government moves to liberalise telecommunications will lead to high prices and will not be in the national interest.

* *Financial Times,* 30th June 1982, BT telephones on sale through rival outlets.
** See, for instance, *Times,* 23rd June 1982, warning of damage by unapproved telephones.

- **Postal services.** Under the 1981 Act the Post Office's monopoly can be suspended, and has been, to allow private operators to run express mail services, for charities to deliver Christmas cards, and to allow transfer of mail between document exchanges.

- **Cable television.** This is a new area of communications which could be run and administered by either the public or private sectors, or by a combination of both. Although not a true privatisation issue, as there is no public sector organisation to be privatised, it raises many of the same questions.

- **Telecommunications — a comment.** Privatisation in this area, by creaming off the best bits for the private sector, seems bound to lead to higher prices being charged by BT for the remaining basic services. And as was said in an LRD pamphlet in March 1982: the supply of equipment by other manufacturers 'may not hurt British Telecom very much, but will almost certainly lead to an increase in imports at the expense of British firms who now supply the equipment to BT'.*

Manufacturing

Diverse areas of public sector manufacturing have been privatised. They are collected together here for convenience:

- **National Enterprise Board (NEB).** The 1980 Industry Act reconstituted the NEB as part of the *British Technology Group* (with the NRDC) and gave the Secretary of State for Industry more power to direct its activities. Under these powers it has been directed to concentrate on helping high technology firms, firms in the assisted areas and small businesses. Once viable, firms must be returned to the private sector. Substantial sales of shares owned by the NEB have already been made.

  The NEB's drive to seek out high technology firms has not been an unqualified success:

  > *High technology drive 'disappoints'* — Financial Times 6.7.82
  > The Californian "venture capitalists" hired by the National Enterprise Board more than 18 months ago to seek out new high technology businesses in the most depressed areas of England claim the project is not going well.

* *Labour Research,* March 1982, pp.58-9: The assault on the nationalised industries.

Mr Jack Melchor, who runs his own $15m fund from Los Altos, south of San Francisco, and who is one of the leading venture capitalists in the area, says he is "disappointed" by the early progress of the £2m Anglo-American Venture Fund, a wholly-owned National Enterprise Board company.

Venture capital companies, which finance high risk businesses by taking equity stakes, are relatively new in the UK, but have grown rapidly in number in the US over the last ten to 15 years.

Mr Melchor teamed up with the NEB, now merged with the National Research Development Corporation into the British Technology Group, in November 1980.

A joint venture capital organisation, which he manages through a jointly-owned management company, was subsequently set up to provide a combination of "seed corn" investment capital and an entrepreneurial management approach aimed at fostering fledgeling ventures in advanced technology, particularly electronics.

Its activities are restricted to the English assisted areas, parts of the country designated special development and intermediate areas.

The management company is authorised to seek out opportunities to transfer to the UK high-technology products, already launched successfully in the US.

Twenty months from its formation, the £2m fund has committed a little over £1m of which £900,000 for five projects has been taken up. Mr Melchor says he has not "seen any attractive propositions in months". Only one investment has been made in the last year.

In addition to a "dearth of good entrepreneurs" in the North of England, where the fund has been concentrating its attention, Mr Melchor says it is proving difficult to manage the fund from the West Coast of America.

A small NEB team does the preliminary vetting of applications, though Mr Melchor is personally responsible for all recommendations to the fund's board.

Mr Melchor, who admits that he may be biased as a result of the steady flow of good projects crossing his desk in California, is negotiating to establish a £10m private fund in London which can invest anywhere in the UK.

Mr Arthur Ward, director of regional affairs for British Technology Group and a member of the Anglo-American Venture Fund board, said last night that progress since the launch had been "quite speedy" compared with other venture capital funds.

The development of the present scheme is being discussed, "but if we have encouraged him to set up on a wider basis in the UK then I am delighted".

● **Steel industry.** The privatisation approach taken has been for joint private sector/public sector ventures to be set up, the so-called *'Phoenix'* companies. Phoenix 1 was set up by BSC and GKN in February 1981 as a means of 'rationalising' wire rod and bar production. The resulting 50/50 owned company trades independently of the parent companies as Allied Steel and Wire.

Phoenix 2 was to have covered the engineering steels sector and to involve agreement between BSC and several private sector companies, but some of these withdrew early on in the discussions and in February 1982 the crucial negotiations between BSC and GKN collapsed, although both agreed to review the position in the future.*

BSC have also made proposals, apparently under pressure from the Government, for contracting out some non-production jobs in steelworks. After strikes it was agreed by the unions at Corby that private contractors could provide canteen and scrap handling staff, but proposals for other plants and other jobs to be privatised have met strong criticism from the unions. As Bill Sirs pointed out "The result is that BSC's tonnes per man-shift figures look improved while all that is happening is that they are shifting the paperwork around" — a common government motive for privatisation throughout the public sector.

- **Rolls Royce and British Leyland.** Both of these companies are often quoted as candidates for privatisation, but recession in the airline and motor industries means that neither is a viable private sector proposition at present.

  However, the 1980 Industry Act transferred responsibility for BL from the NEB to the Department of Industry, where civil servants have allowed the company to divest itself of unwanted subsidiary activities without detailed consideration of the social consequences. The sale of the Bathgate agricultural machinery activities to a private sector company was the subject of a Committee of Public Accounts Report (HC407 of 1981-82).

  It has also been suggested recently that Honda might take a shareholding in BL to bring the companies closer together.**

- **Atomic energy.** All the shares of *Amersham International,* formerly called the Radiochemical Centre Ltd., a firm dealing in man-made radioactivity and sophisticated medical equipment, were owned by the UK Atomic Energy Authority until the sale in February 1982.

  The shares were offered at 142p per share and the offer was

---

* *Financial Times,* 13 February 1982, Steel privatisation project collapses.
** *Financial Times,* 19th July 1982, p.1.

heavily over-subscribed: commission paid to merchant bankers for professional advice was £310,000. The deal illustrated another pitfall of privatisation. It was recently announced that the firm had increased its profits by 109 per cent in 1981-82, significantly higher than forecast at the time of the share offer.

It had been suggested that shares in *British Nuclear Fuels Ltd,* might also be sold off after they were transferred from the UK AEA to the Secretary of State for Energy, but he said in November 1981 that there was 'no present intention' to do so.*

● **British Aerospace.** Reconstitution of British Aerospace as a public limited company was the sole purpose of the British Aerospace Bill, which was enacted in May 1980. The intention, Keith Joseph said, during the Second Reading of the Bill, was for the Government to retain a large stake but *not* to exercise control through its two part-time directors. He went on:

> "The purpose of the Bill is to establish a stable partnership between public ownership and private ownership which we hope will endure over the decades ahead.'**

In February 1981, a limited number of shares were available to employees (just over 3 per cent were taken up) and 100 million shares were offered to the public. The outcome was that 48½ per cent of the shares are now held by private investors who subscribe £148.6m and the remaining 48½ per cent are held by the Government. Net receipts from the sale were about £43m.

Whether the Government's hopes for a public sector/private sector partnership will be sustained in practice is obviously open to debate. The new vertical launch version of Seawolf is indeed being privately financed. But British Aerospace will be expected to finance development of new aircraft and missiles from private sources and this may prove impossible unless co-operative ventures, probably with foreign contractors, are set up.

AUEW-TASS has warned against the grave damage which could be done to the industry if totally private funding is maintained. Early in 1982 it published a policy statement on *The Future of British Aerospace* outlining its fears and some alternative proposals for collaboration between British Airways, Rolls Royce and British Aerospace.

* HC Debate, 16th November 1981, c110.
** HC vol.974, c.213-6.

● **British Shipbuilders.** The company announced plans to reduce its workforce by 1,500 in an attempt to keep losses in 1982 within the limit set by the government which has been reduced from £25m in 1980-81 to £10m.*

Local Authority Services

The position of local authorities contracting-out services was described in the Treasury Economic Report in the following way:

> The decision to contract-out the provision of services is the responsibility of individual local authorities. However, they are being encouraged seriously to consider doing so, as a means of reducing costs to their ratepayers while still maintaining their standards. The Government have been helping by providing information; they have published a report,** commissioned from consultants, which examines pricing and service delivery arrangements across a wide range of local environmental services. Local authorities are increasing their experience of contracting out; some (such as Southend, Eastbourne and Peterborough) have already contracted-out their refuse disposal services, and at least a hundred others are considering doing so.

Although relatively few councils have actually put out services to private contract, and the experiences of those which have, have not always been happy (as in Southend in the snow), increasing numbers are considering doing so or are asking for tenders. An extensive list is given at the back of the TUC's education course book on privatisation.

The services most frequently proposed for privatisation are refuse collection, cleaning, catering and building maintenance, but school meals, housing management and even auditing*** have also been put forward.

In February 1982, the TUC began its campaign to oppose privatisation of local authority services and quoted the report prepared for West Lindsey District Council showing that the savings in Southend from having private cleaning contractors were

* *Financial Times,* 16th July 1982, British Shipbuilders plans job cuts.
** Service Provision and Pricing Policy in Local Government, Coopers and Lybrand study. HMSO £12.
*** Coopers & Lybrand have the largest single share of this market for Local Authority audits its — see Accounting Bulletin, Vol.1, No.1, Michael Lafferty Publications Ltd., 1982.

over-stated by a factor of 10. Both the TUC and the unions concerned have also quoted the ACAS Report, which shows that 'workers in the contract cleaning industry are amongst the lower paid in the labour force'.* The GMWU and NUPE at their annual conferences passed motions opposing privatisation.

Some of the possible union (and media) responses to a privatisation move, in this case refuse collection in Wandsworth, are illustrated by the newspaper extracts reproduced on the following pages.

As the LRD pamphlet on privatisation says of the contracting-out of local authority services:

"Many of the savings claimed are illusory or exaggerated, and privatisation does not automatically save ratepayers' money. It does, of course, mean more profits for the companies providing the service."**

Stop the erosion of local services.

*   ACAS Report No. 20, Contract Cleaning Industry.
**   LRD: Public or Private; the Case against Privatisation: May 1982. See also NUPE paper, on p.46.

Extracts from the *Financial Times:* **Privatisation proposals in Wandsworth, 1982**

● **Initial union response — mass meeting:**

Council faces strike in refuse service row. Financial Times
8th April 1982

The Tory-controlled London Borough of Wandsworth faces a one-day strike by its 6,000 employees on April 19 over proposals to allow private companies to collect refuse.

A mass meeting yesterday of the council's eight unions called the protest action. It may be followed by an all-out strike by about 200 refuse workers, and selective strikes by other groups.

Union leaders walked out of the meeting with Mr Christopher Chope, the council leader, last night. It had been called in an attempt to avert a confrontation.

The unions want the council to withdraw plans to call tenders over refuse collection and discuss an alternative offer of further efficiency steps in the present direct labour service.

Wandsworth became involved in the controversy over "privatisation" of services after it gave a street cleaning contract to Pritchard Industrial Services.

Some national public service union leaders hope the Wandsworth workers will put up stiffer resistance to privatisation than has so far been seen.

● **Strike of 6,000 manual and non-manual workers: indefinite strike of dustmen and switchboard operators:**

Dustmen call strike over private contractors plan — Financial Times *20th April 1982*

Council Services in the Tory-controlled Borough of Wandsworth were at a virtual standstill yesterday as 6,000 manual and white-collar workers staged a 24-hour strike over the council's plans to use private contractors for refuse collection.

The council's 200 dustmen and switchboard operators have decided to strike indefinitely from today.

Workers from private companies will clear the rubbish and operate switchboards during the strike. Council leader Mr Chris Chope said yesterday: "By taking action the council's refuse collectors are making our case out for us. If we decide to bring in private contractors this would be the last time they could hold us to ransom in this way".

In February, the council became the first in London to hand street cleaning to the private sector when it gave the contract to Pritchard Industrial Services.

The council's eight unions called the one-day strike after Mr Chope refused to give them assurances that the council would withdraw the plans to go private. The unions say the present system of the council employing its own workers can be made to run more efficiently.

Only essential services to the house-bound and needy were working yesterday, as libraries, parks, cemetaries, swimming baths and council offices closed.

● **Use of private contractors to break strike: accusations of violence:**

Council's private cleaners 'intimidated' — Financial Times, *5th May 1982*

The private company employed to clean streets in the London Borough of Wandsworth has alleged that a growing campaign of "violence and intimidation" is being directed against it and its workers.

Mr Christopher Chope, leader of the Conservative-controlled council said last night: "There is no doubt that intimidation is taking place. There have been a number of incidents involving flying pickets. We are co-operating with the police as far as we can".

However, leaders of the borough's 200 dustmen — presently on strike in protest against the Council's decision to ask for tenders for cleaning the streets — deny allegations of violence. They have called for a "Day of Action" by workmen from other boroughs in support of their strike.

Mr Dennis English, a strike official, has said that allegations of violence being offered to crews working for Pritchard Industrial Services, the private company brought in during the strike, are "totally ridiculous".

Pritchard lists a series of incidents over the weekend which include; the damaging of hydraulics on one truck, and the cutting of the fuel lines and theft of the ignition keys from another. Several road sweeper trucks had sugar poured into their petrol tanks and there were reports of intimidation of temporary women street cleaners.

Mr Eric Meecham, managing director of Pritchard, said last night: "We are continuing to do our duty in the face of this mindless, vicious campaign".

Mr Chope said last night that the dustmen's strike was a "political" one, in preparation for the borough elections.

He said that the Council had adopted the policy of putting out a variety of services to tender, including tender by the existing workforce. The contract for works maintenance had been won by the staff in that department, he said.

● **Threats of sacking ignored: union support:**

Private services battle may halt council work — Financial Times, *24th May 1982*

Services in the London Borough of Wandsworth face complete closure within two weeks as a long-running dispute between the council and unions over privatisation of many services comes to a head.

A meeting today of the 250 dustmen on strike for the past five weeks is likely to vote to ignore a council instruction to return to work immediately or face the sack.

The decision by a council sub-committee to sack the dustmen is to be ratified by the full council meeting on Thursday. If it goes through as expected the two major blue-collar unions, the General and Municipal Workers' Union and the National Union of Public Employees, will recommend the 2,500 council manual workers to begin an all-out strike.

The GMWU and NUPE, each meeting in conference this week, have issued separate calls to their members to resist measures to hive off services to the private sector and are prepared to back strike action wherever councils push through such measures against union resistance.

Mr Ron Keating, NUPE assistant general secretary said: "There is no way we are going to allow private contractors to come in".

Mr David Basnett, the GMWU general secretary, said yesterday, "If other councils pursue the same line as Wandsworth, then they may also be affected by action.

It is not a question of trying to seek efficiencies, which we agree with. It is a question of ideology".

The issue at Wandsworth arose when the dustmen struck against council plans to seek tenders for refuse collection.

Since then the council has employed Pritchard, the cleansing company, which already has the borough's street cleansing contract, to collect refuse on a temporary basis.

Mr Derek Gladwin, GMWU Southern Regional secretary, said that he would be willing to discuss savings and efficiencies in the service if the dismissal notices were lifted.

However, he would not recommend a return to work on the basis of his members putting in a tender against commercial companies.

The NUPE conference voted to support "all forms of industrial action in the borough, to make an official contribution of £1,000 to the strike fund, and to request the TUC to black Pritchard".

● **Agreement for return to work and for withdrawal of private contracts:**

Agreement reached in dustmen's dispute — Financial Times, *29th May 1982*

An agreement aimed at ending a six-week strike by dustmen in the London borough of Wandsworth, and at averting an all-out strike by 2,500 manual workers, was reached last night after eight hours of talks between the local authority unions and Wandsworth Council.

The agreement will be put to a mass meeting of the 220 dustmen on Wednesday. Under it the council will withdraw the private contractors who have handled refuse collection during the strike and the dustmen will return to work on Thursday.

The original cause of the dispute, however, will not be removed. The council still intends to put refuse collection out to tender though existing dustmen will be invited to apply for the contract.

The dustmen walked out when the council announced plans to tender for their work. They refused to take part in tendering.

Their work has been done largely by Pritchard Industrial Services, on a temporary basis. The company has already secured the borough's street cleaning contract.

Another group of workers, the maintenance men in the council's mechanical workforce, tendered successfully for the contract to perform their work.

The Conservative council fought the recent election on a platform of continued privatisation of a range of council services, including parks and baths. The Conservatives were re-elected, though with a reduced majority.

The local authority unions are the General and Municipal Workers Union and the National Union of Public Employees.

They threatened to pull out all manual workers if dismissal notices against the dustmen, which were confirmed by the council meeting on Thursday, were not withdrawn.

The unions also threatened to extend industrial action to other councils with privatisation plans.

The agreement reached last night between council and union officials may be difficult to sell to the dustmen because of the council's intention to continue with privatisation.

- **Details of tenders disclosed:**
Council reveals details of refuse service tenders — Financial Times, *17th June 1982*

Wandsworth's refuse collectors were yesterday given details of the 14 tenders invited by the Tory-run council as part of its plan to privatise refuse collection.

The lowest tender, said the council, was from Grand Metropolitan Waste Services. At £9.3m over a five-year period it would save the council £7.5m. The council said the tender was £2.1m below the figure submitted by the council's direct labour force whose peace formula, submitted after a seven-week strike, involved 50 redundancies out of 216 jobs and the end to restrictive practices.

The dustmen resumed work earlier this month after a strike, peppered with alleged violence against Pritchard Industrial Services which temporarily performed the service. Part of the peace formula was that the unions would be given details of the 14 tenders for the contract.

Mr Michael Hester, deputy leader of the council, said after meeting union leaders: "Four of the contractors offered savings significantly greater than those proposed by even a streamlined direct labour force".

"We have now offered the unions in excess of £1m as an enhanced severance package in the event of us privatising the service". However, these terms, he said, would depend on a smooth hand-over with no victimisation of the contractor.

Further discussions are to be held with the National Union of Public Employees and the General and Municipal Workers' Union.

The tenders and proposed reforms of the direct labour scheme will be considered by the council's Policy and Finance Committee on July 12 and presented to the council on July 13.

● Alternative union proposals:

Refuse collectors in jobs plan — Financial Times, *6th July 1982*

Wandsworth's 216 refuse collectors have drawn up radical proposals for the reorganisation of their service which they say would save the South London council more than £1m a year and lead to the loss of about 65 jobs.

The proposals will be put to the council later this week by representatives from the General and Municipal Workers' Union and the National Union of Public Employees, the two unions involved. The plans are a final attempt to stop the refuse service going to a private contractor.

Last month, the refuse collectors agreed to go back to work after a bitter and sometimes violent seven-week strike against the Tory-controlled council's plan for the work to go private. The stoppage intermittently involved all 2,500 of the council's manual workers and many of the white-collar staff. The only concession the strikers won was the right to examine details of the 14 private tenders for the refuse contract.

The council has announced already that the lowest tender came from Grand Metropolitan Waste Services. The tender of £9.3m over a five-year period would save the council nearly £7.6m.

A joint union official said yesterday that the refuse workers' new plans would work out £300,000 a year cheaper than the director of technical service's plan.

● Postscript:

Wandsworth it to go ahead with its plans to contract-out refuse collection and is to make additional redundancy payments to its dustmen, who have apparently agreed not to disrupt the new contract.*

The National Health Service**

In some areas some services, such as cleaning and catering, have been performed by private contractors for many years. What is new is the deliberate pressurising of health authorities by the Government to contract-out as many services as possible. For

*Financial Times, 15th July 1982; Council wins deal on refuse service.
**See also COHSE Research Department paper p.80.

NUPE picket against union victimisation at Great Ormond Street, Hospital, 1981.

instance, a Tory City Councillor published a pamphlet in April 1982 purporting to show how the NHS could save £300m by putting out estate management, laundry, catering and portering services to private contracts.* In contrast, at the same time, the National Association of Health Authorities in England and Wales was publishing a guide to schemes within the NHS which had improved efficiency and saved money.

A report in the *Guardian* of the 13th July 1982 said that Norman Fowler had been forced to withdraw a draft circular sent out to health authorities by DHSS officials on how they should proceed with privatising services. The withdrawal did not imply that services were not to be privatised, simply that a more acceptable circular would be sent out at a later date.

NUPE has urged health authorities to resist government plans to privatise catering, cleaning and laundry work. Rodney Bickerstaffe quoted a survey at Stoke Mandeville and St John's Hospital, Bucks., which showed that private contract cleaning cost more than the use of direct labour.**

---

* Michael Forsyth: Re-servicing Health: Adam Smith Institute, London, April 1982.
** *Guardian,* 16th July 1982, NUPE call for boycott on contract out hospital work.

The Government's support for private health insurance schemes, as an alternative source of finance is well-known. But a new twist is that at a meeting in London, at the end of June, the British Medical Association's Central Committee for Community Medicine was told that the Minister of Health had said that community physicians have the right to practise privately in addition to their NHS duties.*

The same organisation which advocated the privatisation of NHS services, the Adam Smith Institute, has also proposed solving the problems of the state pension system by privatising *pensions,* that is by individuals contributing to private pension companies as in Chile.**

Other public sector activities***

There are many examples of privatisation in other areas:

- *The Forestry Commission* put up 5,000 acres of woodland for sale in October 1981 and has offered a further 12,800 acres for sale since then.

- A trading fund has been created for the *Ordnance Survey* with the aim of introducing private finance in the longer term.

- *The Manpower Services Commission* have sold restaurants in skill centres.

   But the new head of the MSC has told the Government that he sees no scope for privatising *employment services* — the PER had been suggested as a possible candidate for hiving-off.

- *The Hydraulics Research Station* has been transferred to private ownership.

Conclusion

Many commentaries on privatisation deal for very good reasons with only one or some aspects of it — nationalised industries, or private health insurance, or local authority services, for instance. But when a more extensive list is compiled, as here, it becomes immediately obvious how the privatisation campaign has pervaded nearly every area of the public sector.

---

   * *Financial Times,* 28th June 1982, NHS Staff can practise privately.
  ** Privatising Pensions, Adam Smith Institute, July 1982.
*** See also SCPS Research Department paper p.147.

2. The Struggle for Wandsworth

Ian Scott
(NUPE Full-time Official)

Dave Benlow
(NUPE Branch Secretary, Wandsworth District)

THE FIGHT AGAINST PRIVATISATION

Introduction

Like a number of other London Boroughs, Wandsworth's electorate chose to throw Labour out of office in the Council elections of 1978 and install what appeared to be a "moderate" Conservative administration pledged to keeping rates down, trimming "bureaucratic waste" and selling council houses. There was little inkling at that stage of the hard Thatcherite approach that would later characterise Wandsworth's ruling group, save a promise to the electorate that direct building works would be phased out during the life of the Council.

Although the return of a Tory Council was not the preferred result, the unions in the borough were not unduly worried. For many years all manual workers (other than building workers) had been united under the umbrella of a joint shop stewards' committee drawn from three unions: The National Union of Public Employees; The Transport and General Workers' Union; The General and Municipal Workers' Union. Unlike many other areas of London, there was a high level of co-operation and good relations between the unions. Building workers were represented through their own stewards committee of UCATT.

Among the manual unions there was a feeling of optimism that their organisation could effectively resist the new council should it decide to adopt a harsh approach towards the workforce. This confidence was put into practice during the winter of 1978-79, when selected sections of Wandsworth's workforce were on strike for seven weeks. The action centred on refuse collectors, fitters, boilermen and street sweepers, and it was felt that some valuable lessons had been learnt about the organisation of industrial action.

Within a year of the Tories assuming power in Wandsworth they had achieved power nationally in the election of May 1979 — clearly pledged, amongst other things, to cutting back public expenditure. Almost by way of preparation for this event, right-wing Tories on Wandsworth Council had organised a coup against the existing "moderate" leadership. The new leader, Christopher Chope, was to become an ideologue for the new Tory right, with Wandsworth as the testing ground for a wider-ranging attack on council services, jobs and working conditions.

In 1980 Michael Heseltine, the Minister of the Environment, announced the Government's intentions of massively reducing expenditure in local government by both a reduction and change in the way the rate support grant was distributed, which would divert resources from the cities to rural areas.

By autumn 1980, with Wandsworth enthusiastically embracing the policy of cutbacks, there had been a reduction of over 1,000 jobs through the use of "natural wastage" and frozen posts. This had been contributed to by the closure of some old people's homes, luncheon club facilities and other council establishments considered surplus to requirements.

The dust — privatisation stage one

Knowing the enormous extent of the financial cutbacks they were planning to make, in late 1980 the council began to raise a new element in negotiations with its workforce — privatisation. For some time it had been attempting to introduce new working arrangements into the refuse section. The old bonus scheme was seen as being badly matched to the refuse requirements of the borough. There can be no doubt that events at Southend, where Exclusive Cleaning had made such a public issue of taking over the refuse collection service from direct labour, affected Wandsworth. However, at this stage, Wandsworth did not go as far as to seek private contractors. Rather, they made it clear in the negotiations that unless significant concessions were made, private contractors would be brought in.

They put a time limit on negotiations. Well in advance of that date the council circulated leaflets to all householders in the borough warning them to expect disruption of the service at the appointed date.

The pressure and the propaganda worked. The refuse service

accepted a reduction of nine vehicles and 39 jobs, saving the council over £400,000. The refuse section breathed a sigh of relief as the new agreement was implemented in January 1981. It seemed that the example of Southend was not to be applied to Wandsworth, and the refuse service would operate in the future under direct labour.

Those wishing to leave received enhanced severance payments — there was no shortage of volunteers. No one mentioned at that stage that there was no clause in the new agreement guaranteeing that, as a result of the negotiations, the service would stay "in-house". It proved to be a significant omission.

More cuts

In January 1981, having dealt with the refuse service, Chope announced further intended savings of £21m. He proposed an overall reduction of 300 manual and 400 white-collar posts, in combination with rate and rent increases. This announcement triggered the first signs of joint manual and white-collar workers co-operation in the borough. A combined "day of action" was organised and strongly supported by the membership. Rather than get involved in such a broad struggle at that stage, the council conceded a "no compulsory redundancy" agreement. It still insisted that the 700 jobs would have to go, either through voluntary severance or through re-deployment within the council. From the union's point of view a positive aspect of this critical conflict had been the emergence of a liaison committee between NALGO and the manual unions. It was to prove a very important alliance in 1982.

The street-sweepers — one step further

The council had tested the use of 'privatisation' as a threat and found it beneficial in their negotiations with the refuse section. Taking heart from that, the council turned its attention to the street-sweepers. Street-sweepers had been involved in protracted negotiations with the council about work arrangements and conditions. As a result of these negotiations the establishment had been reduced, but the council was still not satisfied. However, rather than simply threatening privatisation as they had with the refuse, this time they proposed that negotiations with direct labour should run alongside a public invitation for private firms to tender for the work. Despite a considerable union lobby and some supportive industrial action on the day, the Leisure and Amenities Committee decided to support this approach on 1st July 1981.

This was a clear tactical departure on the part of the council and represented its first real attempt to privatise. Nevertheless, the process went ahead and by 15th December 1981 a new agreement covering street-sweepers in the Borough based on a reduced labour force of 100, plus considerable improvements in the flexibility of labour, had been concluded. At that time this already meant the loss of approximately 30 jobs. Simultaneously, however, the public tender invitation had resulted in approaches by 13 contractors. Of the 13, eight had been discarded leaving five "possible" (table 1).

By the time of the meeting of the Policy and Finance Committee in January 1982, the council had narrowed its options to two: direct labour or Pritchards Industrial Services Ltd.

As will be shown in the case of refuse, the approach of narrowing down to only one alternative to direct labour is the best option for the council. It maintains the possibility that direct labour will be chosen to the last minute. The majority of Tory councillors voted to support private enterprise on ideological grounds, but they didn't want to say so too early in the process. This effectively diffuses opposition, keeps employees in doubt about the use of active opposition, as it is hinted that such action would harm their chances of being chosen. It finally presents a decision at the end of a long tendering process, by which time employees' morale is lowered and willlingness to fight the decision reduced.

In response to the choice between Pritchards or direct labour, the union side pointed out the impracticality of the manning levels proposed by the contractor and the lowering of the service that would result. The council, for its part, repeated that they were interested in "value for money" and were not committed to privatisation as a matter of principle and furthermore would not necessarily take the lowest offer.

At its meeting on the 18th January 1982 the council of course opted for Pritchards, which was by sheer coincidence the lowest contractor with the lowest contractor's price and the lowest manning. They were to begin on 1st March 1982.

Any residual trust in the word of the council evaporated as a result of this decision. The award of the contract to Pritchard's caused some serious re-evaluation of the union's approach. However, time for such re-evaluation was very short.

TABLE 1

STREET CLEANSING SERVICE

OUTLINE OF CONDITIONS OF SERVICE OFFERED BY CONTRACTORS

Staff Levels
(Direct Labour 100)

Name of firm	Weekly rate of pay and overtime	Pension	Sickness	Holidays
EXCLUSIVE 74	HGV Drivers (45 hours) £146.25 Other Drivers (40 hours) £128.00 Sweepers/loaders (40 hours) £120.00 *Overtime* Mon to Fri: Time and one third Saturday: Time and half Sunday: Double time Average: £23 per week	Employees are required to joint the scheme and pay 5% contribution. Pension at 1/60th of final salary for each year of service.	Less than 6 months service: NIL. 6 months service and over: 4 weeks full pay 4 weeks half pay	*After 6 months service:* 1¼ days for each month worked *After 12 months service:* 20 working days per year. *Plus* 8 days statutory holidays per year.
RAMONEUR 86	40 hour week Grade A Street Sweeper £80 Grade B Driver/Sweeper £90 Grade C Specialist Driver/ Sweeper £96 Grade D Market Loader/Driver £104 Grade E HGV Driver £110 Overtime as necessary	To be discussed after one year's service.	At Company discretion.	3 weeks per year

PRITCHARD 63	Working week (Mon to Sunday) any 5 days Basic pay (40 hours) £90 Attendance Bonus £20 Performance Bonus £15 Drivers' Allowance £5 *Overtime* Mon to Sat: Time and half Sunday: Double time	NIL.	After 12 months service and up to 3 years: 4 weeks at £50 per week. Over 3 years service: 8 weeks at £50. Free BUPA membership Free Life Assurance.	*In first year:* One day for each 2 months *1 to 5 years service* 3 weeks *5 years and over* 4 weeks *Plus* 8 days statutory holidays.
TASKMASTERS 76	Contract to run on 2-shift basis. 7-hour shift — Mon to Fri: £2.50 per hour for 35 hours inclusive of meal breaks. Gang Bonus: £8 per week *Overtime* Standard week: First 6 hours at basic, then time and third Saturdays: Time and half Sundays: Double time Average £30 per week	Eligible to join at age of 25 years after one year's service. Pension at 1/80th for each completed year.	After 3 months service: 4 weeks basic pay. 4 weeks at half basic. After one year's service: 5 weeks at full basic and 5 weeks at half basic Free Life Assurance	In first year: 15 days Second and subsequent years: 20 days Plus public holidays
HOME COUNTIES 76	Basic Day (40 hours) £110 per week Attendance Bonus £2 per week Overtime available	Pension at least as attractive as local government. 4% contribution.	It is anticipated that local government entitlements would be maintained.	Up to 3 years service: 4 weeks 3 to 5 years service: 4 weeks and 1 day After 5 years service: 4 weeks and 3 days

PLEASE NOTE that the above is a brief summary of what it is understood the named firms would offer. Firm details can only be provided by the firms concerned.

Source: Wandsworth Department of Technical Services.

51

The dust — a second time

On the 19th February 1982 Mr Michael Heseltine, who by this time had announced a further 3 per cent cut in the 1982-83 rate support grant for local authorities, visited the borough. He was taken to see the new street-sweeping firm in operation, met their Managing Director, Peter Fox, and was widely photographed holding a Pritchards' broom in a workmanlike position. In a publicity coup Mr Fox took the opportunity to publicly hand over a letter to Mr Chope, offering to save £5m over the next five years if the refuse service was handed over to Pritchards.

The unions protested strongly about the stage managing of this event. The council said that there was no pre-arrangement but, of course, could not ignore such an approach. As a result of the Pritchards "initiative", on the 28th March 1982 the council decided to invite private tenders for the refuse service and asked the trade unions to "submit concurrently their proposals for improving the cost-effectiveness of the existing direct labour service, including the financial consequences of such proposals".

The council at this stage was obviously acting in a very confident manner. Street-sweeping had been privatised with a minimum of effective opposition. Some action had been taken in their support, based in the mechanical workshops, but it had failed.

The council were now asking the unions to join in a similar process to the street-sweepers, and barter blindly for the jobs of the existing labour force. It is significant to note that the tender process being offered simply means that the normal bargaining arrangements between the union and the employers is completely undermined. It meant the unions being reduced to the status of a private contractor simply trying to offer the lowest possible price to get the job.

Having had the experience of negotiating a new bonus scheme for refuse in January 1981, and then the experience of the street-cleaning tender process, there was some opposition in the unions to simply going the same way with the refuse service. Options were considered. They could put in a bid in accordance with the council's wishes — but against that were the previous experiences and an awareness of the multi-national contractors' ability to submit "loss-leaders" on the basis of totally impractical manning levels, simply to get a foothold. They treated labour as a very cheap commodity indeed and had a very low commitment to the quality of the service. Was it therefore likely that direct labour could win simply by putting in a bid? It was concluded definitely not, especially as it was now plain that the Wandsworth Tories were ideologically committed to privatisation.

In the light of these factors, it was decided that the unions would not join in the tender process, but instead would launch a vigorous campaign of opposition to the whole approach of the council. That campaign would have to begin as early as possible, and would be aimed at being as broad-based as possible, including all unions, ratepayers, Labour Party branches and the local Trades Council. The Liaison Committee between manual and white-collar workers was rejuvenated, and it quickly became clear that there would be considerable support for a struggle with the council. It was decided to press for an end to the tender process and a "no privatisation" agreement covering all workers in the borough. In late March 1982 the Liaison Committee decided to call a meeting of all employees in the borough, both manual and non-manual, at which a recommendation would be put to begin combined borough-wide action on April 19th, the day that the council had stated it was to make a public call for tenders. The unions were to respond with an attempt to stop the whole tendering process and prevent the advance of privatisation into the borough.

The Liaison Committee began a press and propaganda build-up which included press statements, adverts and leaflets. It was decided to contact as many groups locally as possible, including community and tenants' organisations. The local Trades Council had already formed an "anti-privatisation" sub-committee as a result of the street-sweeping difficulties. It now began to prepare supporting materials on the issue of the refuse. Approaches were made to tenants' organisation through the housing sub-committee of the Trades Council, which drew in tenants from many areas of Wandsworth.

A complicating factor was that local council elections were due on May 6th. Regular contact had been established with the Labour Party's Policy Organising Committee. Some concern was put forward from certain quarters in the Party about the possible timing of the action. The unions felt that privatisation was an issue that had to be publicly fought out and did not accept that electoral disaster would be the result of action so close to election day. It was hoped to create a considerable groundswell against privatisation and its consequences through a broadly based campaign, exposing the truth about contractors' poor services and terrible employment policies.

The campaign begins

On the 7th April a mass meeting of over 2,000 Wandsworth employees heard contributions from national union leaders, including Rodney Bickerstaffe, the newly appointed general secretary of NUPE. The meeting overwhelmingly supported an immediate campaign, including industrial action, to begin on April 19th. The unions met the leader of the council on the evening of April 7th, but were told that the council still planned to invite tenders as from the 19th.

From the point of view of the Liaison Committee, it was felt that early action had to be taken, as delays would allow the tender process to get under way without opposition, which could lead to demoralisation and increase the difficulty of organising opposition at a later date. It was further felt that Labour could usefully argue against the dismantling of services during the election campaign. The unions were under no illusions about the real plans of the Wandsworth Conservatives and were convinced that the tendering process was more of a trap than an opportunity.

The action therefore began on April 14th with the aim of stopping the tender process. The unions indicated that if such a withdrawal of the tender process occurred, they would, as normal, be willing to discuss matters with the council, but the privatisation process had to be halted first.

The importance of the white-collar workers and their union NALGO in organising and supporting the campaign was considerable. Contrary to the traditional view that manual workers tend to have of NALGO branches being unwilling to take strong action, the NALGO branch in Wandsworth was respected for its organisation and track record on previous issues in the borough. There is not a shadow of doubt that without the support of NALGO a much weaker campaign would have been waged.

The action began with a one-day strike by the whole borough, followed by selective action organised through the Liaison Committee. From the start, NALGO had their telephonists, cashiers and people in the rating section on permanent strike. The manual side aimed for a one-week strike of all manual staff followed by more selective action. Social services were in the first instance exempt.

From the beginning the action began to gain marked support and publicity. The width of the action was considerable, and largely flowed from the decision to try and achieve an end to privatisation for all workers in the borough. Privatisation had been positively identified as a threat to all employees and the campaign was seen as having possible benefits for all. Details of the extent of the action are shown by an official report to the Establishment Committee of the council:

TABLE 2

Supportive action against privatisation

REFUSE DISPUTE

Summary of Industrial Action

1. On April 19th strike action was taken by 1,550 officers and 420 manual staff.

2. Since that date strike action has been maintained by the manual staff in the Refuse Section, and strike action has been taken on various dates by the following staff:

Administrative staff	(12 officers)
Computer staff	(14 officers)
Finance Staff	(14 officers)
Refuse Inspectors	(8 Officers)
Supplies staff	(5 officers)
Telephonists	(18 officers)
Boiler Operatives	(2 manual staff)
Caretakers	(52 manual staff)
Cemetaries staff	(29 manual staff)
Drivers — Mobile Library/Ambulance Service	(30 manual staff)
Hall Cleaners/Attendants	(4 manual staff)
Highways/Sewers staff	(24 manual staff)
Mechanical Workshops staff	(55 manual staff)
Messengers	(9 manual staff)
Parks staff	(26 manual staff)
Pool Attendants	(13 manual staff)
Stores staff	(11 manual staff)
Traffic operatives	(26 manual staff)
Transport/Depot staff	(18 manual staff)

3. Other industrial action short of a strike and in breach of contract has been taken in the period April 28th to May 13th by various office staff in the following departments:

Administration Department	68 staff
Housing Department	145 staff
Planning Department	36 staff
Social Services Department	33 staff
Technical Services Department	14 staff

Source: Report to Establishment Committee of the Council, 27th May 1982.

Ninety per cent of NALGO members stopped work on the 19th. It was very encouraging to see white-collar staff taking a leading role in putting pressure on the council. It was impossible to telephone the Town Hall and the council's rates were left uncollected. On the manual side, approximately 1,000 were out for a week, from parks, public halls, public conveniences, catering, sewers, transport.

There were some problems, however, especially as regards the fitters in the mechanical workshops. They had been the focal point of resistance to the council's earlier proposals to privatise the street-sweeping service. They too had been faced with the threat of privatisation. The previous October they had gone back to normal working on the basis of a "no-strike" clause and were busy cutting staff to try and ensure that their work stayed "in-house". They saw their interests threatened by involvement in the stoppage and although they joined in from time to time, their requests to the Liaison Committee for exemption became a depressingly regular feature of committee meetings.

Overall, however, the first week was seen as very successful from the union point of view. White-collar workers and manual workers established their own strike committees, which would then report their plans to the overall joint Liaison Committee to be sanctioned or not.

Picketing

It was the refuse section that provided the main pressure and initiative on picketing. All refuse collectors were expected to picket and from the beginning the refuse section held the view that the issue could not simply be fought in Wandsworth. They saw themselves as being the first in a long line of dominoes, and if they were privatised others would very soon follow. This has in fact proved to be the case with neighbouring Tory Borough of Merton having now decided to use Taskmasters to carry out their refuse and street-sweeping services, and Hammersmith and Kensington and Chelsea considering going the same way.

Having decided that the issue was a broad one, the manual

workers' strike committee began sending out pickets to other boroughs to seek support. Although this led to a number of meetings in the boroughs, it did not lead to widespread support. With noteable exceptions like Southwark and Lambeth, there was in general a reluctance on the part of the workers in the other boroughs to become involved. However, the approaches made elsewhere did have a positive side. In addition to raising the dangers of privatisation and beginning to make branches elsewhere consider their response, there was a very clear impact on Wandsworth council. From the beginning of the stoppage it had brought in private contractors to try to minimise the effect of the strike on the streets of Wandsworth. As a result of sending pickets elsewhere, and with the support of the GLC as far as their refuse tips were concerned, the contractors found that they were unable to get rid of refuse they had collected. The unions attempted to push them as far out of London as possible. With the longer and longer journeys to find private tips, they were unable to control the situation in Wandsworth. They were finally pushed as far as Dartford in Kent, and of course this began to cost the council considerable amounts of money in contractors' fees. As a result of successful picketing, a number of private contractors withdrew and the impact of action in the borough began to shine through more strongly.

Publicity and propaganda

From the beginning considerable emphasis had been placed on the need to begin to get the message about privatisation across to all union members and the public both inside and outside Wandsworth. A four-page newspaper was produced under the name "Wandsworth Call", devoted to the issues of privatistion and the reasons for the action. Leaflets both for the membership and the public were produced and distributed widely. A full-page advertisement in the local newspaper was bought and proved successful. Every effort was made to respond to press calls and requests for interviews, etc. The industrial action was providing the platform from which the issues about privatisation were very publicly debated. As is always the case there was some criticism of the type of coverage given by the media, but the unions' tactics of speaking on the subject at all times, whether it be press, radio or television, continued and successfully raised the issues about privatisation on a wider scale than had been achieved elsewhere.

WANDSWORTH CALL

A paper produced by London Borough of Wandsworth (manual workers) Joint Shop Stewards Committee **APRIL-MAY 1982**

OUR SERVICES UNDER ATTACK

THE WANDSWORTH Conservatives have declared war on their employees on the eve of the council elections

It is nothing more than a cynical election gimmick. They are trying to make the trade unions the scapegoats for their mismanagement of the borough's finances and the terrible neglect of services.

They have the cheek to say that the trade unions are making a 'political issue of privatisation'. But we didn't introduce privatisation: it is THEIR political football, not our's.

For the past few years we have co-operated with the council in making savings which have included the loss of 1,500 jobs.

No one can accuse the trade unions of not playing their part, especially when you consider the level of unemployment that exists in Wandsworth and the cuts in services that this involved.

But the Tories are never satisfied. They want more. Now they want to destroy the jobs of:

- 220 dustmen
- 50 vehicle mechanics
- Parks and gardens employees
- Housing caretakers
- Public halls employees
- Town Hall employees

OUR fight is for our members' jobs, our members' living standards and our members' conditions of work.

But more than that — WE ARE FIGHTING FOR THE PEOPLE OF WANDSWORTH AND THE SERVICES THAT THEY HAVE A RIGHT TO EXPECT.

It is our job to carry out this fight, and it is not political, except insofar as we are fighting employers who are politicians.

The Tories are using privatisation to destroy our jobs and living standards. But did you know that 20 years ago they decided that contractors should not be employed by the council?

It's a fact: the Conservative Party kicked Surridge's, the refuse contractors, out of Wandsworth because of the lousy service that they provided!

Most of the facts have been hidden from the people of Wandsworth — We want you to know the truth.

If we lose our battle, it won't be only us that lose:

- Services will be slashed still further
- Unemployment will rise dramatically because contractors never employ enough people to do the job properly
- The Conservatives will have laid the ground for massive rate rises for the future because of the contractors ability to hold the council to ransom.

WE ARE COUNTING ON THE SUPPORT OF ALL THE PEOPLE OF WANDSWORTH IN OUR FIGHT!

Front page extra

SINCE the end of Pritchards two-month trial period sweeping Wandsworth streets
- a staggering 500 complaints a week are pouring into Council offices.
- Pritchards have been fined an average of £1,000 each week for streets not swept.

They are proving our argument. Wandsworth residents are saying: Pritchards cannot do the job.

Councillor Chope knows these facts and he is hiding the truth from the ratepayers. When will this fraud end?

Missing streets

- The Council forgot to tell Pritchards about the existence of 69 streets in Wandsworth.

How much more will local ratepayers have to fork out to foot the bill?

Getting the message about privatisation across to all union members and the public.

The local elections May 6th

Up to the local elections on May 6th the unions' tactics remained the same. NALGO continued to play a crucial part with the selective action of telephonists, cashiers etc. The council had responded by bringing in agency telephonists, but NALGO had replied with instructions to all their members not to pick up telephones. The manual side continued to centre on the refuse collectors, with supportive action by housing caretakers, parks and other sections.

The election was seen as an important focus for both the unions and the existing Conservative council. Wandsworth was seen as being rightfully Labour territory, with the takeover by the Conservatives on the previous round of council elections something of a disaster. Other London boroughs in the previous round, who were seen as being in greater danger, had stayed Labour, but Wandsworth, regarded as a "safer" area, had swung to the Tories. Considerable debate had taken place inside the borough about the causes of this situation. It is impossible here to go into this debate, but suffice it to say there were hopes on the union side that Labour would regain power and indications had been that they might win by a small majority. An additional unforeseen factor was of course the problem of the Falklands, which many people felt was affecting the elections in a significant way. Whatever the influence of the Falklands, the outcome of the election was that the Tories retained control, albeit with a reduced majority. Wandsworth was one of the few Boroughs where there was a swing to Labour, but of course, this was of little consolation as the power remained where it had been before. The Conservative majority had been reduced from 11 to 5. The SDP/Liberal Alliance had a disastrous night in Wandsworth, achieving only one seat and leading to great local gloom amongst SDP/Alliance supporters.

Negotiating positions

Up to the local election of May 6th the unions had been pressing for an end to the tendering process and a "no privatisation" agreement. The Tories had maintained a studied silence in terms of responding to the claim. They had joined in the debate about privatisation publicly, but had no formal meetings with the unions to discuss resolving the impasse.

Clearly the result of the election changed their view of things and

Demonstration, Wandsworth, 10th May 1982, at the height of the battle against privatisation.

also affected the position of the unions' campaign. On the union side some people had put more importance on the outcome of the election than others. For everyone it was a setback, but in the case of NALGO it resulted in strong pressure from their membership to withdraw from the campaign. Financial problems had begun to affect them also, as they had been paying their strikers from local funds. A number in the NALGO leadership felt that they should grasp the nettle of not paying strikers, but their active part in the campaign came to an end at a mass meeting on the 12th May 1982, when they voted to return to work and open negotiations with the council. NALGO's decision was not heavily criticised, as it was generally recognised that they had taken their members a long way in the struggle with the council. Those NALGO members who had been on selective strike for three weeks were beginning to feel isolated and were not convinced that it was within the union's power to win the dispute.

Despite this there had been a demonstration in the borough on May 10th, organised through the unofficial London Local Authority Joint Shop Stewards' Committee. Over 1,000 people had joined the march through Wandsworth, which had given a considerable boost to those unions who remained committed to fight on.

It was in this context that the negotiating positions of both sides changed. The council initiated the change by breaking the veil of silence through the new Deputy Leader, Maurice Heaster. The new council wanted an end to the strike and were to make an attempt to draw the unions back within the parameters of the tendering process. The manual unions, with the loss of the NALGO arm, felt that it was an impossible proposition to simply continue to demand an end to tenders and a "no privatisation" agreement. The tendering process had begun on April 19th and by this stage the council were receiving responses from private contractors. However, the unions remained committed to not joining in the tendering process and wanted to retain their freedom to negotiate. It was decided on the union side that the aim should change to demands to see the outcome of the tendering process in terms of the details and costing put forward by the contractors, and then require negotiations about keeping the service in the hands of direct labour. The tendering process was due to close on June 2nd.

After approaches from Councillor Heaster, meetings began to take place between the two sides. Mr Heaster emphasised the

Wandsworth dustmen picket at Feathers Wharf over private contractors being hired, April 1982.

serious concern of the council about the continuing action. The manual strike committee emphasised its opposition to the use of private contractors and wanted the details of all tenders after the closing date, and negotiations after they had been supplied.

On May 19th the council put forward terms for a possible "return to work" agreement (see table 3). It amounted to an extension of the closing date for tenders to allow the unions to put their own proposals. Additionally the council introduced a new concept into the negotiations i.e. buying out the opposition of the existing workforce. They indicated that improved severance terms would be available "in the order of £800,000".

TABLE 3

Mr I. Scott,
Area Officer
National Union of Public Employees,
13/15 Stockwell Road,
London SW9 9AT

LONDON BOROUGH OF
WANDSWORTH

19th May 1982

Dear Mr Scott,
I write to confirm the outcome of today's discussions between the Chairman of the Establishment Committee, his Deputy and Vice-Chairman and the Trade Union Side.

The Chairman stated that the Council is prepared, on a return to normal working, to enter into immediate negotiations to assist the trade unons with cost reductions in the present service and, to allow further time for these negotiations, is prepared to extend the date for the opening of tenders by two weeks beyond June 2nd to allow for the conclusion of these negotiations.

In return for an immediate resumption of work the Council is also prepared to enter into negotiations on improved severance terms, which will cost of the order of £800,000, in the event of a contractor being retained for the service.

The Council rejected a proposal from the trade unions for negotiations to take place with the Council to be commenced after the opening of tenders and in comparison with the figures then submitted. This proposal cannot be agreed as it would undermine the fairness of the tendering process by disclosure of the lowest tender.

As a resumption of normal working was not agreed at the meeting the Chairman stated that unless there is a return to normal working by Monday 24th May, authority will be sought from the Council for dismissal notices to be issued to employees who are in breach of their contracts of employment with the Council.

Yours sincerely,
L. Evans,
Chief Personnel Officer

By this stage the action that was being taken in the borough was losing some support amongst the manual staff. It was decided to adopt a new tactic of closing down the council depots altogether with particular attention to the central depot. Outside the borough, whilst knowledge of the dispute had spread across London, little in the way of supportive action was being taken. Also, on a wider scale, the national conferences of both NUPE and GMWU were due to take place. Members of both unions lobbied their respective conference and received strong support. The NUPE conference voted overwhelmingly to support the action and decided to encourage official supportive action from other branches.

It was in this context that the May 19th "offer" from the council was rejected. At this stage the council remained unwilling to disclose the details of tenders as, in their view, this would undermine the "fairness" of the tendering process. Councillor Heaster also gave notice that unless a return to normal working could be agreed by May 24th, authority would be sought from the full council to dismiss all strikers.

The General Secretary of NUPE, Rodney Bickerstaffe, wrote to all individual councillors making clear the union's support for its members and warning against any sackings.

Nevertheless, on May 24th, the council confirmed the authority of the Deputy Leader to dismiss the men still on strike. However, it was plain that having taken the power to do so, the council were reluctant to take a step that could provoke considerable response due to the number of dismissals involved. Unfortunately, by this stage, the Wandsworth strikers were very tired and the level of action in the borough had gradually reduced to centre on the refuse collectors only. This isolated position was one which the unions had attempted to avoid. They had been at pains to prevent the dispute being labelled simply as a "dustman's" dispute.

The balance of forces at this stage led to lengthy negotiations about a formula for a return to work. This was finally reached on the 28th May 1982 and accepted at a stormy meeting of the refuse section.

Return to work and beyond

The agreement to return to work included provisions to supply the unions with details of the tenders after the closing date (June 2nd). In addition the director of the department dealing with the refuse was to come forward with his own plans for the refuse department. The unions were given the right to negotiate about the contents of the director's proposals, but not to change the overall level of savings that he was aiming at.

Finally, the unions had the right to include their own independent proposals to go before the council. Negotiations were also to take place on possible redundancy and severance payments on the clear understanding that much more money was on offer. The council were definitely interested in buying off further opposition to their plans.

Judged against the original aims of the campaign this was a far from satisfactory position to reach. However, in the circumstances prevailing by that time, it was seen as the best possible option. The council were clearly pleased, as they had succeeded in dragging the dispute back within the confines of what they saw as the tendering process. Despite severe setbacks the unions had avoided being dragged into the tendering process and intended to continue the struggle against the council's proposals. On June 16th in accordance with the return to work agreement, the details of the tenders was given to the union side (table 4). It straightaway became clear, and was confirmed by the council, that Grandmet was the main contender for the job. They submitted proposals which gave the lowest manning (133) and the lowest annual cost (£1,993,038). It was immediately plain that the direct labour force could not and would not compete with such a submission. It would have entailed impossible reductions in manpower and vehicles, and the service would have suffered.

After considering the position that had been reached, the unions decided that they would draw up their own proposals which would be presented to the council and the public as the most efficient method of maintaining a satisfactory level of service in the borough. A policy decision was taken not to try and undercut the contractors. Rather, the unions would stick at a level that would maintain the service in the borough. Value for money for Wandsworth ratepayers was put forward as being best achieved through an improved direct labour service. Propaganda against the contractors centred on the very poor showing of Pritchards' street-sweeping service and the level of penalties incurred. In addition to drawing up their own scheme, the unions also prepared their own submission and criticisms of the contractors' proposals to go before the council. Throughout this approach the underlying theme

TABLE 4

REFUSE COLLECTION TENDER — MANNING LEVELS

Contractor	Personnel		Supervision
	A	B	
Waste Management Limited	132	—	1 Manager 1 Superintendent 3 Inspectors 1 Tele/Clerk 1 Clerk
Taskmasters Limited	163	124	1 Project Manager 2 Quality Control (Domestic) 1 Quality Control (Non-Domestic) 1 Admin Officer 1 Clerical 1 Storeman/Assistant
Exclusive	—	112	1 Manager 3 Area Managers 3 Admin Staff
Grandmet	133	—	1 Manager 2 Superintendents 1 Clerk/Book-keeper
Drinkwater Sabey	not quoted		3 Management 4 Supervisors 4 Admin
Boiler and General	not quoted		8 Supervisory 5 Admin
Factory Cleaners	152	121	Not stated
Wastedrive Limited	162	149	1 Manager 3 Supervisory 2 Admin
Pritchards	146	115	1 Contract Manager 3 Supervisors

Source: Wandsworth Department of Technical Services.

'A' and 'B' refer to two types of tender contractors may have made. 'A' is based on a site existing style of service. 'B' refers to any proposals for a new style of service.

TABLE 5

REFUSE COLLECTION SERVICE

OUTLINE OF CONDITIONS OF SERVICE OFFERED BY CONTRACTORS

Name of Firm	Weekly rate of pay and overtime	Pension	Sickness	Holiday
WASTE MANAGEMENT LTD.	Driver/Loader (40 hrs) = £141.52 Loader (40 hrs) = £135.84 Weekday and Saturday Overtime = Time and a half Sunday = Double time	Membership of National Freight Consortium Scheme available to all staff.	Less than 6 months service: NIL 6 months to 1 year = 10 weeks 1 to 2 years = 15 weeks Over 2 years = 20 weeks at £45 per week/£9 per day *Personnel Insurance Scheme:* Medical Severance: 3 weeks pay to 15 weeks depending on service.	4 weeks per year *Plus* 8 statutory holidays'
TASKMASTERS	Loaders £130 Drivers £140 Gang Supervision £150 Shunter/Assistant (1) £100 *Overtime* Saturdays = Time and a half Sundays = Double time	Eligible to join at age of 25 years after one year's service. Pension at 1/80th for each year of service	*After 3 months service:* 4 weeks basic 4 weeks half basic *After one years' service* 5 weeks at full basic 5 weeks at half basic	In the first year: 15 days Second and subsequent years: 20 days *Plus* Public Holidays.
EXCLUSIVE	Driver (HGV) (45 hrs): £155.50 Ganger (40 hours): £137 Loader (40 hrs): £135 *Overtime* Mon to Fri Time and one third Saturday Time and one half Sunday Double time	Employees are required to join the scheme and pay 5% contribution. Pension at 1/60th of final salary, for each year of service. Free life insurance cover.	Less than 6 months: NIL 6 months service and over: 4 weeks full basic pay 4 weeks half basic pay.	First year: 15 days Subsequent years: 20 days *Plus* 8 days statutory holidays per year.
GRANDMET	40 hrs (Mon to Sun) over any 5 days Driver (HGV) *Basic* £90, *Bonus* £25, *Holiday accrued* £2, *Total* £117. Co-driver (HGV) *Basic* £88, *Bonus* £24, *Holiday accrued* £2, *Total* £114.	The Company's Pension Scheme is 'contracted out' of the State Scheme. Employees are required after 5 years service and if qualified by age, to join the Company's Payroll Staff Pension Scheme.	Less than one year: NIL 1 to 3 years: 2 weeks 3 to 5 years: 4 weeks over 5 years: 6 weeks Paid at the rate of: First 4 days of absence in an 8-week period, normal basic pay.	*Annual Holidays:* 2 days after 4 weeks service. graduating to 20 working days after 48 weeks service. Thereafter 20 workings days per year. Plus Statutory holidays.

TABLE 6
WANDSWORTH BOROUGH COUNCIL
Refuse Collection Service
Details of existing staff and outline of conditions of services

Existing Staff	Weekly Pay	Fixed Bonus	Total	Holidays	Sickness Payments		
					Years Service	Entitlement in weeks	
						full pay	half pay
Foreman G	£98.50	£39.94	£138.44	6 months to 4 years: 20 days	½		4
Loader/Driver Class I G	£90.90	£39.94	£130.84	5th year onwards: 25 days	1	4	8
Chargehands F	£93.05	£39.94	£132.99	Plus 11 days statutory or extra statutory days	2	8	13
Loader/Driver F	£88.45	£39.94	£128.39		3	13	16
Shunter drivers F	£88.45	£39.94	£128.39		4	16	20
Refuse Collection E	£84.90	£39.94	£124.84		5	20	20
Labourers B	£77.50	£39.94	£117.44		6 and over	26	26
Total establishment 216	Includes London allowance						

Collectors Basic £85, Bonus £24,
Holiday accrued £2, Total £111
Overtime
Mon to Fri Time and half
Saturday Time and half (when not part of working week)
Sunday Double time (when not part of working week)
Special re-call, split duty, rest and night work rates also are paid

After 4 days, pay at 50 per cent of basic

Shorthand Pay — Authorised when a crew is incomplete, based on — one man short — 12 times basic hourly rate plus one days bonus for one man to be divided between the remaining members of crew. When two men are short the calculation is based on 24 times the basic hourly rate.

Pension — Employees are required to join the scheme and pay 5 per cent contribution. Pension is at 1/80th for each year of service plus lump sum of 3/80ths for each year of service.

of the unions was that an attempt to "compete" with contractors on their own terms was a blind alley and a practical impossibility given a commitment to maintaining the standard of the service and the conditions of service of the directly employed staff. The issues of efficiency and value for money were therefore directly related to what the unions fixed as an acceptable level of service in the borough.

Final negotiations also took place on severance terms with local union representatives. The tactics of the council were to link higher severance pay with guarantees of no further disruption of the service. They finally offered 2½ times statutory redundancy pay plus one week's pay in lieu of notice for each year of service (maximum 12 weeks). The stewards accepted.

Out to contract

From the council's point of view, by this stage, they had laid the ground for a decision to use contractors. The unions' position was that they had put forward an efficient and "value for money" proposal linked to a satisfactory level of service in the borough. This was done with an eye to the future campaign about the service. Accordingly on July 12th the crucial committee meeting took place which had an extensive set of documents before it:

a. An evaluation of the tenders by the Director of Technical Services which had been supplied to the trade unions. Appendices to the document including revised working arrangements based on proposals put forward by the Director of Technical Services; an outline of conditions of service offered by contractors (table 5); details of severance and early retirement terms; letters to the council from Exclusive Cleaning; Pritchard Industrial Services Ltd., and Taskmasters.

b. Trade union submission plus proposals.
    Comments by officers of the council on the trade union submission.

On July 12th the Committee predictably took the decision to employ Grandmet to do their refuse work and this was confirmed by the full council meeting on July 13th.

Immediately following that meeting the council wrote to all refuse collectors indicating that their last day of service would be September 17th. This was questioned by the unions under the terms of the Employment Protection Act and the council had accordingly to amend that date to October 13th. In reply in an attempt to undermine any savings that the council might obtain from the contractors, a claim under the Fair Wages Resolution 1946 was lodged with the Department of Employment. The unions were able to do so as a commitment to that Resolution was included in the tender documents. The unions were hopeful of making progress in this area as the proposed wages to be paid by Grandmet for refuse collectors and drivers were inferior to those being paid by Pritchards for street-sweeping.

Carlos Augusto (IFL)

Pritchard moves in.

More privatisation

It is also important to note that at the meeting on July 12th/13th, in addition to privatising the refuse collection service, the council also decided to review all other services in the borough with a view to possible privatisation. So far, consequential threats of privatisation have begun to appear in negotiations on housing caretakers' conditions and the employment of certain parks maintenance workers. With the council decision, the dispute in terms of direct action by the unions terminated. The membership felt that there was little scope for changing the council's mind and the focus should move to exposing the failures of the contractors and the type of service they provide.

Since that time, on information received from the council, 150 refuse employees have been interviewed by Grandmet. Of those, 72 men have been offered a job on much inferior terms to direct labour. Needless to say, none of the shop stewards or union activists have been employed, but a small number, who signed a council list to return to work during the dispute, have. The final position is that Grandmet will probably employ far more than the 133 people they proposed. Wages and conditions are as outlined in table 6. Wandsworth council are receiving 150 to 200 complaints daily from residents who are dissatisfied with the quality of refuse collection achieved by Grandmet. The NUPE submission to the Fair Wages Resolution is still pending. NUPE also applied for recognition to Grandmet.

LESSONS AND CONCLUSIONS FROM WANDSWORTH

The Threats

Many of the tactics and arguments adopted by Wandsworth council may well be used by other employers with the same aims in mind. If the unions are to successfully confront the threat, there are a number of lessons from the dispute that may be of wider relevance. First, they should understand the nature of the *threats* facing them.

1. The political threat

The present Conservative Government is very dogmatic about its preference for private enterprise as opposed to public provision of services. This attitude has permeated many local authorities under

Conservative control. In such authorities private contractors are seen as being better than direct labour as an article of ideological faith. Contractors are attractive and welcome to the new Tories — they are closely linked to the Government's policy of cutting expenditure and services; they are cheap because they cut jobs, wages and conditions of service and have no commitment to maintaining any standard of service; they are seen as essentially a weapon against the unions. They are traditionally anti-union or under-unionised firms; they tend to rely more on casual labour and are thus difficult to organise. So they further the Conservative aim of weakening public sector unions, and indeed the union movement as a whole.

Given these considerations, an early evaluation that any workforce must make is the type of political employer it is dealing with when the issue of privatisation is raised. If it is Thatcherite, then the unions' approach must be based on the clear understanding that direct labour has little support and indeed will face active opposition from its employer. Old conceptions of amicable negotiations no longer apply. Wandsworth learnt this the hard way and had already suffered the reversal of the street-sweepers before doing so.

2. The threat of blackmail

Privatisation proves an economic threat to members not only through the existence of private contractors who employ many fewer people at much reduced conditions of service, although that is serious enough. It also poses an even wider threat where it is used as a bargaining weapon by employers in an attempt to bargain away terms and conditions of direct labour that have taken many years to build up. This has happened in a number of areas and in the Wandsworth case operated successfully in the refuse section, where they initially gave up nine vehicles and 40 jobs in response to the threat.

3. The threat of low pay

Privatisation also goes so far as to threaten a method that has been relied upon by unions in many areas to achieve reasonable wages, i.e. work-study based bonus schemes. In NUPE's biggest sections of membership, i.e. health and local government, they have been used since the 1969 National Board for Prices and Incomes Report on Low Pay recommended them as a method of overcoming the terrible wage levels of most NUPE members. Whilst the approach has not overcome the problem, many members now rely on bonus earnings to achieve anything approaching a living wage.

However, with privatisation the concept is now developing of "tender-related bonus schemes". This means, in effect, that employees will have their proposed bonus scheme based not on work-study but on what price the contractor can do the job for. This 'cash limit' approach to schemes with the limit set by contractors will, if it gains ground, undermine the original aims of bonus schemes and make low-pay an even more serious problem. Demands for flexibility of labour and job cuts related to schemes will be much stronger than before.

The lessons

Given the very serious nature of the threats implicit in "privatisation", considerable thought needs to be given to the campaign in response to that threat. A number of possibly useful points have arisen from the Wandsworth experience.

1. Lessons for organisation

(a) Early organisation

Wandsworth found out in practice the amount of time and effort required to prepare for a campaign. The lack of knowledge amongst both the membership and the public at large about privatisation is massive. It is therefore essential that the job of education is started as early as possible, whether or not the threat of privatisation has actually been brought forward by a particular employer. In Wandsworth we suffered from having to press forward without sufficient groundwork due to the time scale involved. Education of the membership is particularly important as in a number of cases we found that some members do not see the prospect of employment with contractors as a threat. This complacency needs to be overcome by bringing home what happens in practice. Large numbers of ex-direct labour employees are not taken on and those that are, are vulnerable to "hire and fire" policies and very poor conditions of service.

(b) Organisation on a broad front

The issue of privatisation needs to be fought with as broad a front of support and co-operation as possible. A particularly important element in such support should be the consumers of the services, the ratepayers. They are a crucial pressure group and can add significant political pressure behind a campaign. Efforts were made in Wandsworth through public meetings and contact with tenants associations to try and mobilise that support. But such attempts were made hastily and with insufficient groundwork to really bear a great deal of fruit. Again it would be much more useful for branches to form links with consumers as early as possible. There is no doubt that alliances of this type will provide a strong basis for pressuring employers who propose run-down of services through the use of contractors.

Further important elements in the width of the campaign must clearly be other unions, trades councils and local Labour Parties. In the experience of Wandsworth we should not under-estimate the extent of the work that needs to be done inside the Labour Party. It would be wrong to assume that Labour councillors will automatically support an anti-privatisation campaign. Many Labour representatives are privately, and some not so privately, attracted by the Conservative arguments about saving money. In the case of Wandsworth it was not until a number of meetings had taken place with the Labour Group and Party branches that the Party openly committed itself against privatisation. Involvement of the Labour Party and education of its members in the fight against privatisation should be an essential part of the campaign.

Finally, it is essential to break down any barriers that exist between white-collar and manual unions. Privatisation is blind to the different coloured collars that jobs require. They are all equally threatened. In Wandsworth NALGO proved to be an essential ally in mobilising and carrying on the campaign. From the Wandsworth experience it is clear that the threat extends to all. At the same meeting that privatised the refuse collection service, the council took a decision to review all services with a view to possible privatisation. To get maximum union support against privatisation it is therefore wise to pursue initially a "no privatisation" agreement covering all workers covered by the employer. This type of umbrella approach attracts broad support and certainly helped to begin the Wandsworth campaign on the correct footing.

(c) Membership organisation and education

A further important aspect of overcoming feelings of isolation is to ensure that the members' own unions are fully briefed and their support organised. In the case of Wandsworth the national executives of the NUPE and GMWU made the action official from the beginning. This was re-enforced by national conference decisions later in the dispute. But, of course, most unions have regional structures and efforts should be made to ensure that all union members in the immediate region are fully behind the struggle. Getting your union behind you is a simple message, but to some extent it is one that was not fully carried out in the Wandsworth case, to the detriment of the campaign. Outside Wandsworth the industrial action had the immediate impact of raising other members' awareness of the dangers that privatisation poses. Other councils will have noted the amount of disruption that was related to a decision to try to privatise. Such disruption is a "cost" as far as any council is concerned. It is a cost in terms of council time, effort and resources in countering the union opposition and trying to maintain public support for their own point of view. It is likely that these "costs" will be taken into account by councils that are not completely ideologically committed to privatisation and may serve to direct some from the path of ridding themselves of direct labour. The costs will appear on the "debit" side of the equation when employers are considering the options. This again emphasises the need for early organisation to ensure that any employer is aware of the strength of opposition that is likely to arise if a proposal to privatise is made. The Wandsworth Council were in the event willing to pay considerable sums of money over and above statutory redundancy pay to "buy off" continued opposition and try to ensure a smooth transition to private contractors. They even paid backlog money after the dustmen returned to work, to the tune of £85,000 in spite of the fact that contractors had been in the borough during the dispute. Given the type of council that Wandsworth has become, it will be appreciated that the money was not given for altruistic reasons.

2. Lessons about industrial action

Obviously a very important element of consideration in any campaign will be whether or not industrial action should be used and, if so, when it should be used. A decision in this respect must hinge on an evaluation of the type of employer being dealt with. If the union is facing an ideologically committed employer then the campaign must recognise this from the beginning. In the case of Wandsworth clear evidence had been given by the experience with street-sweepers as to what the unions were up against. This decision can only be made locally in the light of local knowledge and experience, but it should be borne in mind that the longer that a response is delayed, the more difficult it will be to organise one, as morale tends to fall as the issue gets drawn out by a tendering process. In Wandsworth the Council were happiest when there was no industrial action and they had changed the union back to trying to influence the decision by written submissions.

In Wandsworth's case the industrial action proved itself to be an essential platform around which the arguments about privatisation could be effectively brought out and fought out in public. There are, however, some points that should be made about the width of the action. The original aim was to involve as many unions as possible in support of the campaign on the basis of the broad approval previously described.

In the event, inside the borough this initially worked well due to the "umbrella" nature of the claim for a "no privatisation" agreement. Over time the width of the action began to fall away as many members felt that they were unable to put sufficient pressure on the council to change its policies. Eventually this led to the isolation of the dustmen. Avoiding such a development had been at the forefront of our priorities.

To overcome this type of situation the involvement with local trades council and private sector unions is crucial. The Wandsworth trades council was closely involved and did a great deal of supportive work, but the support and activity only extended as far as the trades council activists. At all times the only action being taken was by public sector unions inside the borough. The aim should be to achieve supportive action from private sector unions in the area. This raises the whole issue of how to convince the private sector unions of the need to act to defend public sector services. It will require a great deal of work and effort to break down the barrier between the public sector and the private. The trades council is the forum in which to begin to do it. The rewards can be an effective method of putting further pressure on a Conservative council through the impact on private employers in the area. If there is a decision to take action therefore, do not leave out approaches to private sector unions.

3. The lessons for a campaign against privatisation

The broad aim of any campaign is of course to defeat privatisation, but special emphasis should be given to convincing the people locally of the real arguments against privatisation.

(a) Defining "efficiency" and "value for money"

In Wandsworth the Conservatives publicly maintained that they were not pursuing privatisation out of any political ideology, but simply because they were seeking "efficiency" and "value for money". This will be an argument wherever privatisation is proposed for local services.

A number of union members, ratepayers and some Labour Party representatives may be swayed by these arguments. It is almost inevitable that ratepayers will be initially attracted by arguments which involve spending less money.

This is an area that must be tackled clearly and openly. Indeed it is an essential task for the union to expose the myth that many Conservatives and contractors themselves are trying to make an accepted fact; that contractors mean efficiency combined with cheapness and good value.

The facts from the Wandsworth experience are that contractors are in practice *more inefficient* than direct labour. They cannot guarantee that the *level of the service* is maintained. They are cheaper simply because they cut conditions of employment and do not employ enough people to get the job done satisfactorily. But even with their lower costs there must be doubts whether they will be cheaper in the long run. Once they have gained control of the services it is quite likely they will start *increasing their prices.*

In Wandsworth the report on the first six months of street-sweeping has confirmed that there is a *poor service;* the contractors use "hire and fire" methods and in general have a haphazard approach to the job with little planning or training involved.

It is essential to break down the Conservatives and contractors' attempt to identify "cheapness" with "efficiency and value". This can only be done by exposing the terrible services that contractors give and the way contractors treat their employees. To do it effectively the unions need evidence rather than opinion, facts rather than accusations. *It is crucial for the union to monitor the performance of contractors in areas where they have been successful in forcing their way in.*

Apart from that, it is also essential that we formulate our own definitions of "efficiency" and "value" and approach the ratepayers with those definitions.

(b) Attacking the contractors

During the dispute in Wandsworth an important element was the embarrassing information brought forward about Pritchards as a company. Their type of employment policies, their services and lack of experience were all used to good effect. Clearly an avenue of approach should be to campaign not only against the employer who proposes to use contractors, but also the contractors who intend to offer themselves for use. As much information and propaganda as possible should be circulated as widely as possible. Many of the companies are national or multinational in nature and there is undoubtedly a lot of possibly damaging evidence about the previous work they have been involved in. It needs to be collated and publicised.

Also the nature of competition between contractors may be usefully exploited. They seem only too ready to criticise each other and point at each other's shortcomings. A good example is the letter from contractors sent to Wandsworth council at the time it was to take its decision. Exclusive Cleaning criticised the wage rates being put forward by Grandmet. Pritchards in their letter revealed that they were worried by union accusations of bad conditions. Taskmasters were upset because their "plastic bag" approach was labelled as "unsafe".

4. Lessons about the tendering process

(a) The dangers of involvement in the tendering process

One lesson from the events in Wandsworth is that the employer will do everything to try to get the workers involved in the tendering process. By joining in, the workforce is reducing its own position to that of the private contractors and accepting their definitions of "efficiency" and "value". It is foolish and naïve for any union to have faith in the tendering process as a method of saving jobs. The multinational contractors they would be competing against have no commitment to the service and are able to stand temporary losses. The only thing they want is to get hold of the potential for future profits.

(b) The dangers of accepting confidentiality

The employer will maintain that it would, of course, be unfair to the tendering process to allow the unions to look at what contractors are saving. Confidentiality becomes a sacred principle of tendering. The confidentiality is necessary to the employer; without it the vast majority of direct employees would quickly discover that they cannot "compete" with tenders put in by the big private contractors and that they are very likely to be made redundant. This would cause action by the workforce early in the process, which the employer wishes to avoid. So the tactic of the employer becomes that of maintaining the lie that the direct workforce has a chance.

(c) The danger of unrealistic hope

A management strategy may be to narrow down the options to direct labour and the contractor they have already chosen, and to keep those two options open as long as possible. By stressing this phoney confidentiality the employer may succeed in keeping the hopes of the workforce alive until the very last moment. When the final decision comes in favour of the contractor, those that have been involved in the tendering feel it is too late to do anything. Also, morale is undermined as a result of the long-drawn out process and the divisive arguments within the union what to do about the offer of severance pay, and what levels of job loss should have been offered to be "competitive".

An important lesson is that the workforce may get unrealistic hopes out of becoming involved in the tendering process. From a trade union point of view it is essential that they realise the real position early on.

(d) The danger of temporary success

It is not safe to conclude that where negotiations for improvements in services from direct labour have already taken place successfully, the threat of privatisation has been avoided. A good example is the Wandsworth refuse collection service where, due to political pressures, a one-year-old agreement was ignored and contractors were still adopted. A suspension of the tendering process is not as good as stopping it.

(e) Negotiations instead of putting in a tender

Stopping the tendering process should of course be the first aim. However, where a trade union does not have the power to do this, it still does not mean that putting in your own tender is the only alternative. Collective bargaining is a much better and more democratic way to express trade union organisation than putting in a confidential tender. Trade union branches that are not able to stop the tendering process may be well advised not to join it, but to wait until it is finished. After the closing dates proper negotiations about definitions of efficiency and services could take place on the basis of detailed information provided by the employer about the tenders submitted by private contractors. Tendering blind for your own job is degrading and will leave a litter of crestfallen trade union negotiators.

Conclusion

In conclusion, then, from the Wandsworth experience it is plain that the use of privatisation poses the most serious of threats to the unions and their members. It is an extension of the Government's policy of cutting public expenditure and public services. But, in addition to simply being a cuts policy, it attempts to go to the root of union power and influence by bringing in anti-union and under-unionised firms. It threatens jobs, wages and conditions. Even where contractors are not brought in, they help the employer brow-beat employees into giving up manning levels and conditions that have taken many years of bargaining to establish. It threatens to institutionalise even more the existence of low pay in the public services. It is part and parcel of the Government's policy of lowering the level of such services. Finally, and just as seriously, the use of the tendering process attempts to undermine the recognised bargaining role of a union and reduce it to a blind barterer for jobs.

The policy of privatisation can be successfully opposed but it requires a broad campaign, early organisation and determined resistance. Further, as it flows from political ideology supporting the interests of private enterprise rather than public services, it cannot simply be fought individually. The Labour Party has an essential role to play in linking up with unions at all levels to campaign and expose the realities of privatisation. Serious efforts must be put into organising the support for public services amongst those who use them. Privatisation cannot be allowed to remain simply a public sector issue. It fundamentally affects the type of society we live in. If public needs are to be adequately met in the future, privatisation has to be defeated now.

3. The NHS

(Confederation of Health Service Employees (COHSE) Research Department)

Introduction

Privatisation in the National Health Service takes many forms, and this perhaps makes it more difficult than with other industries to appreciate exactly what is happening. The present Government has admitted that it would like to see a quarter of health service care in this country provided by the private sector.* In fact, this represents barely the top of the iceberg of this Government's plans for the privatisation of the NHS.

Privatisation of the health service includes the following different aspects:

1. Government expenditure plans, which result in cuts in services in the NHS.

2. Government legislation and health service directives which promote an independent sector.

3. Government policy on the contracting out of NHS services; and on the use of agency staff.

4. The expansion of private medical insurance schemes and the growth of the market.

5. The increase of private medical developments.

6. The popularisation of the last two.

Government policy towards the NHS

During the 1979 General Election campaign Mrs Thatcher said her party had no plans:

> "to make people pay to visit their doctor, no plans to introduce hotel

---

* *The Times,* 23rd June 1980.

charges for those in hospital and we shall not reduce the resources devoted to the Health Service.''*

She also said that prescription charges would not go up.

These election pledges now make farcical reading. Patients do not actually have to hand over money before their doctor consents to see them, nor do they yet have to physically pay for their hospital beds; but certainly the ideals and aims of a free comprehensive health service, as envisaged in 1948, are increasingly thwarted and negated by this Government's policies.

The Thatcher Goverent wasted no time in cutting back resources for the NHS. Successive Budgets, and expenditure plans enforcing strict cash limits, have meant drastic reductions in the level of services and in employment in those services. The Government claim to have increased manpower in the NHS. However, skilled and experienced NHS workers continue to be unemployed. In June 1980 4,199 SRNs, SENs and SCMs, 3,965 nursing auxiliaries and assistants, and 4,893 hospital orderlies were registered unemployed.**

Furthermore, from the time the Tories took office up to September 1981, 182 hospitals were completely closed and 345 were partially closed or suffered change of use of departments. In one twelve-month period from 1980 to 1981, 5,768 hospital beds were lost through hospital closures alone, resulting from these policies.

Tragically, people's expectations are short-lived. The overall effect of cut-backs in the NHS has been that people now accept that the state service does not offer as much today in many areas as it did a few years ago. Inevitably this means that some will look towards a glamorous new private sector.

In spite of the election pledge that prescription charges would not go up, it took only two months for Mrs Thatcher's Government to more than double them, and in the three years since 1979 prescription charges have gone up by 550 per cent. Charges for dental and optical treatment and to road accident victims have also been increased, by at least 45 per cent. The increase in health service charges is part of the Government's policy to reduce confidence in a state-provided service and to emphasise their point

* *Nursing Mirror,* 26th April 1979.
** Department of Employment *Gazette,* August 1980.

that free health care is not a right. Gerard Vaughan described a free health service as "undesirable and unrealistic".*

Moreover, in line with true Tory thinking, the Government is trying to shift the burden of paying for health care away from the general public, directly on to the consumer. In this way, those who use the service most, i.e. the chronically sick and the elderly, pay most.

At the same time an attempt is being made to turn people away from the long-established principle of a publicly funded service by trying to get them to raise money for health care through their own efforts. The 1980 Health Service Act actively encouraged health authorities to raise money through street collections, bazaars and bingo. The Act has been described as a charter for private medicine. It abolished the Health Services Board, thus ending the phasing out of pay beds from NHS hospitals. It also empowers the Secretary of State to make NHS services and accommodation available to private patients and to authorise private practice in NHS hospitals where demand requires it.

In their promotion of the private health sector, the Tories know that they have their strongest allies in some members of the medical profession. It did not take long for the Government to capitalise on this. One of their first actions on taking office was to introduce new contracts for NHS consultants, allowing full-time NHS consultants, for the first time ever, to undertake private work without damaging their NHS status.

Other directives and health circulars have confirmed the Government's intention to promote the private sector. Examples include:

1. Amendment to the Land Transactions procedure to enable Health Authorities to give priority to the private health sector before land or buildings are put out for sale on the open market.**

2. Confirmation of amendments to the Health Services Act which refer to the use of NHS hospital facilities by private patients.***

3. Removal of restrictions on Health Authorities' use of private agency staff and the encouragement to Health Authorities to plan future health services with the private sector.

* *Hansard.*
** HC (80) 4 April 1980.
*** HC (80) 10 December 1980.

4. Advice on the management of private patients in NHS hospitals.*

In June 1980 a draft health circular was issued, suggesting that health authorities should consider ways of contracting out building maintenance work, catering, non-emergency aspects of the ambulance service and laundry work. The circular also hinted that the Government was thinking of building hospitals in the future without laundries, so that all laundry work would have to be done privately. At the time Gerard Vaughan said:

> "there is nothing new in the use of outside contractors by the NHS. We are, however, encouraging Authorities to explore the possibilities more widely than has been the case."**

In August 1981 Gerard Vaughan wrote to all Health Authorities in order to review the use of outside contractors. The response was mixed, although the Secretary of State tried to emphasise that all Health Authorities contracted out at least some services. Since then the Government has been trying to promote the use of outside contractors on the grounds that they are more efficient and economical and should produce savings. In June 1982 they issued the now controversial health circular urging Health Authorities to contract out catering, cleaning and laundry services if they could be provided more cheaply by the private enterprise. However, Norman Fowler later denied that the circular had been issued and emphasised that the plan was not to be implemented. This denial contrasted with a statement made by Geoffrey Finsberg, a Junior Health Minister, in the House of Commons to the effect that a circular would be issued urging Health Authorities to seek private tenders very soon.

The contracting out which currently takes place appears to be dominated by a few private firms, some of which are connected with the hospital development companies. A survey conducted by COHSE amongst its regional membership shows that some Health Authorities do contract out such services as cleaning and works maintenance. Crothalls, a private cleaning firm, which is part of the Pritchard Services Group, appears to hold most of the contracts for cleaning and domestic services. Pritchards is the firm which has taken on private contracting for a number of local authorities, including street cleaning in the London Borough of Wandsworth.

---

* HC (82) 7 March 1982.
** *Guardian*, 15 March 1980.

Another prominent cleaning company is Grand Met which is part of one of the private hospital development groups.

Growth of the independent health sector

Traditionally the bulk of private health care in Britain was carried out in NHS pay-beds or in private clinics, and paid for from an individual's personal resources. This is no longer the case; private health care at the moment is an expanding concern with £330m a year business.* This is largely due to the recent and rapid emergence of private health insurance companies and private hospital development companies, aided by this Government's policies, and given much encouragement and publicity by the mass media.**

The private health market is dominated by three large American development companies: Humana, America Medical International, and Hospital Affiliates International — who own such prestigious hospitals as the Wellington, the Harley Street Clinic, the Princess Grace, and the Princess Margaret.

There are also three health insurance companies — BUPA, Private Patients Plan (PPP), and Western Provident Association — which between them control about 97 per cent of the market. It is estimated about 1.5m people*** in Britain are now covered by health insurance schemes operated by the three main companies. Six per cent of the population are estimated to be in family schemes. However, the majority of health insurance is now based on group schemes, and the trend is towards employer-paid group schemes. PPP estimate that 60 per cent of their new business now comes from group schemes.

The survival of health insurance schemes and medical development companies depends on the continuance and growth of group insurance. Interestingly, an incentive to join work-based health insurance groups was given by the Government in a recent Budget. The 1981 Budget abolished the tax on subscriptions to health insurance schemes for employees earning less than £8,500 a

---

* Estimate made by Lee Donaldson Economic Consultants in 1981.
** Gerard Vaughan said in the House of Commons in March 1981:
   "It is our policy to encourage the development of the private health sector, and we welcome investment in the field whether from the UK or abroad."
*** Lee Donaldson Associates: 'UK Private Medical Care Provincial Scheme Statistics'.

year, thus giving workers an incentive to join schemes. The employer also is able to have the cost of 'buying' health insurance for his employees off-set against gross receipts for profit purposes. The formation of group schemes not only lowers the group subscription rate for each contributor, but also ensures (depending on the size of the group) insurance cover for high risks, that is people who probably would not have been insurable on an individual basis.

Churchill Hospital, Oxford, 1982. What will privatisation mean for him?

A. Nicola

A typical insurance scheme provides cover for hospital accommodation (to a limit), professional fees (to a limit), in-patient drugs, radio-therapy, X-ray and physiotherapy. It would not generally cover any out-patient care and drugs, general practice, dental care, optical care and many types of treatment.

What people do not usually realise is that when they are most in need of health care, private medical insurance will not cover them. Pregnancy, confinement, abortion, accidents, geriatric care, mental handicap and psychiatric conditions, or any chronic sickness are not generally covered by private insurance.

However, such has been the success of the health insurance companies and the private hospital development companies that outside organisations and companies are attracted to invest in the private market. Trafalgar House and British Caledonian Airways have been involved in discussions over the building of a private hospital near Gatwick Airport. The Grand Metropolitan Hotel Group are in the process of building a private hospital near Bath at a cost of £5m. United Medical Enterprises Ltd, substantially owned by the NEB, wanted to build a private children's hospital next to the world-famous Great Ormond Street Hospital. Traditionally cautious institutions like the banks and insurance companies are also entering the market. A group of Yorkshire businessmen has been backed by the Legal and General Insurance Company, Friends Provident Association and the Merchant Bank to build four private hospitals in West Yorkshire. The Midland Bank has backed Seltahart Holdings Ltd to build four private hospitals. BUPA recently sought permission to build a £5m hospital at Portsmouth in addition to their new developments in Manchester, Cardiff, the Wirral, Bushey and Harpenden. Hospital Corporation International, part of Hospital Corporation of America which is registered in the Cayman Islands, is building a 100-bed private hospital in Southampton — opposite the City general hospital.

The private sector now has more than 140 acute hospitals, with more than 35,000 beds, including 6,500 surgical beds. Kensington, Chelsea and Westminster Health Authority has the greatest concentration of private hospitals, with a total of 1,271 beds. The Authority is always short of about 1,200 key staff — especially nurses.

Why the NHS must be defended and privatisation opposed

The NHS must be defended in principle in the first place, because, despite its deficiencies, it provides medical care for people according to their need rather than their ability to pay directly for its services.

Furthermore, the NHS is not just a sickness service. An often neglected function of the NHS is its role in health education and preventive medicine. The NHS has also made dramatic improvements in health research, in the eradication of many diseases, and in increased care and life expectancy for the elderly and handicapped, who because of these advances demand more of its services. It is doubtful whether the range of services and treatment provided by the NHS could even be contemplated by commercial enterprises. No other type of health system could cope with the complexity and volume of work that the NHS does, and it is doubtful if many would even try, on the grounds of unprofitability. Health is a major business in the private sector — based, as it is, on quick turnover and profit maximisation. But health should not and must not be a commodity for sale, dependent on the individual's purchasing power to obtain the best.

One of the most serious consequences for health care provision that the existence of a private sector brings out is the perpetuation of the belief that there are two kinds of service. The best is for those who pay or who join a private insurance scheme, and the second best is for those who 'have to' rely on the state. There is no justification for this kind of belief. However, the deliberate creation of the idea of a two tier system effectively condemns those people who cannot afford, or do not want, to buy their treatment to a second class, and thereby inferior, service.

Private medicine benefits only the very rich, the private medical companies who are out to make a profit and the doctors and surgeons who do private work. This is the very antithesis of what the National Health Service stands for. The NHS is not concerned with making a quick profit and reserving the best and quickest treatment for those with most money. As Aneurin Bevan said:

> "The essence of a satisfactory health service is that rich and poor are treated alike, that poverty is not a disability and wealth is not an advantage."

One of the most serious aspects of the existence of a private health sector is the division of medical care. The private sector concentrates, 'creams off', the most specialised acute cases where there might be most professional interest and which can be treated relatively quickly and for an arranged fee. The cases requiring more on-going treatment and long-term care do not attract the interest of the private sector. Yet these kind of cases represent the areas of greatest health care need. In this respect the NHS becomes the

Cinderella Service, left with the care of the chronic and long-term sick. Viewed this way it is in the interests of the private sector that the NHS continues — as little more than a second-rate back-up. Furthermore, private practice creates a bias that ensures that those in greatest need have to join the longest queues and suffer most. The harshest effects of the unequal distribution of doctors and resources — away from the industrialised working-class areas and to the suburbs and the south-east — fall on those least able to complain — the uneducated, the low paid and the institutionalised sick — precisely those areas least covered by medical insurance schemes and of least interest to the private sector.

The private medical sector has been artificially cushioned. It has been allowed to thrive and grow at the expense of the state sector, at a time when the NHS has been deliberately cut back and restrained. For example, private health companies now negotiate with Health Authorities to buy up NHS land or hospitals, including facilities and equipment, which have been forced to close because of cut-backs. Since the Government's guidelines on this were published in April 1980 this practice has become widespread. In one year, 1981, the Government was estimated to have received £15.5m from land sales (despite the embarrassing example of Robrayston Hospital, Glasgow, which was sold for £400,000, only for the purchaser to resell in a matter of weeks for £4m). The Government expect the 1982 receipts from land sales to be much higher. It is insidious to see NHS facilities deteriorate or made to close because of cut-backs, whilst the private sector is able to spend £20m on glamorous hotel-like buildings, or to buy for a song former public facilities, many of which are conveniently equipped and ready for use.

The cumulative effect of constant cuts and lack of resources in the NHS inevitably means not only a deterioriation in state services, but also a real reduction in the level of services. Unhappily the private sector is able to cash in on this, because, while accepting a depleted state service, some people will look towards the private sector for their needs. The existence of a glamorous private sector, thriving at a time when the NHS is not, also has a damaging effect on the morale of overworked staff struggling to cope in increasingly strained situations. Under these circumstances it is not surprising that some staff are attracted over to the private sector, which promises better working conditions and the opportunity to do the job for which staff have been trained. This has grave consequences for the state sector; it means a loss of scarce manpower trained at state expense, and familiar with NHS organisation and routine. It also causes difficulties in recruiting staff, particularly in areas of high private concentration, like London, where there is direct competition. This of course has a further cumulative effect on the staff loyal to the NHS who find themselves coping in even more constrained circumstances. The result could be longer waiting times and reduced patient care. Agency staff are usually viewed with suspicion by the permanent staff and trade unions; and particularly if changes in personnel are frequent, they may have a disruptive effect. They are also very costly. Last year the employment of agency nurses cost the health service £30m.

The question of state-trained staff working in the private sector raises other problems. At present, the majority of medical staff are trained by the NHS and at Government expense. The private sector hives off these staff without making any contribution to their training. This is contrary to the attitude of the medical profession as expressed recently by Sir Douglas Black, the President of the Royal College of Physicians:

> "I am concerned about the present rate of growth of the private sector. This is because I believe a doctor whose education has been largely at public expense should give some return by devoting the greater part of his /her time to the health service, not through compulsion but through a sense of service."*

Some of the private health companies are thinking of introducing their own training courses, but this in itself raises problems. If the private sector is to have its own training schemes, what will happen to the present guaranteed standards of training and level of proficiency, and will health education become the subject of competition?

Developing its argument on NHS expenditure policy further, the Government is insistent in its attempts to introduce the contracting out of NHS services, on the grounds that it will produce savings of up to £300m out of the approximate total of £3bn which the NHS spends on hotel and general services. However, the case has never been proved and the figure should be viewed with caution. Contracting out of services has not been shown to be more

---

* Quoted in LRD publication: "Public or Private, the Case against Privatisation", May 1982.

economical, nor more efficient, and there are relatively few major contracts for ancillary work. Private companies are likely to put in an initial tender, on which they will accept low or zero profits, so they can put in a bid with which the NHS cannot compete. They are able to do this because they are nearly always part of multi-national organisations which can withstand losses in some areas. However, once the contract is secure, they are likely to put up their charges — or lower the standard of service. Furthermore, it is grossly unfair to compare tenders which have been costed using different methods of accounting, or where different numbers of factors are costed.

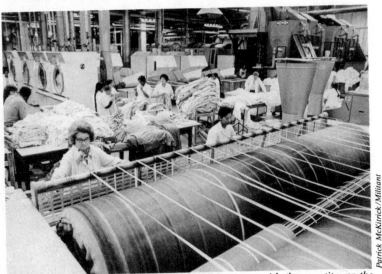

A hospital laundry: '. . . the private firms cannot cope with the quantity, or the time-consuming cleaning, of heavily fouled linen.'

Even health managers now admit that the contracting out of services is more expensive than direct labour. A survey at Stoke Mandeville and St Johns Hospital, Buckinghamshire, where cleaning services are contracted out to Crothalls, has shown that cleaning by the private firm cost £897,600, £78,900 more than the cost using direct labour. Crothalls have over £6m-worth of NHS cleaning work, but have recently been dropped by Essex Health Authority because of the cost. Outside cleaning firms are also notorious for shoddy work. Attempts to contract out laundry work have proved inefficient. Laundry is put to outside contractors in the Isles of Scilly and Penzance at an estimated cost of £2,000 per week. But the private firms cannot cope with the quantity, or the time-consuming cleaning, of heavily fouled linen. The NHS handles millions of items of laundry a year — a medium-size hospital can generate 70 tons of laundry a week.

Despite the experiences of Health Authorities who have put out services to private firms, the Government seems likely to introduce further directives urging the use of outside contractors. No matter how diluted a directive is, nor how innocuous the contracting out of cleaning may appear at first sight, the use of contractors must be opposed. It would mean further losses of NHS staff, and is simply another attempt to privatise the service. If allowed to take hold, this would become the launching pad for the contracting out of other services, including care and other support services — whilst still under the umbrella of the NHS. This would be the beginning of the fragmentation of the state service, and a golden opportunity for the private sector to take over.

Those who believe in the NHS must demonstrate the effects of privatising the health service. They should be aware that, although privatisation is done on a piece-meal basis, a very sturdy private sector has developed alongside the state service, challenging its existence. It is necessary to point out the dangers of private medical practice and to underline the inadequacies of private health insurance schemes. If the expansion of the private sector is allowed to continue, we shall not be progressing into an era of technological medicine with patients cared for in luxury rooms. Instead we shall be regressing to the state of affairs that existed before 1948, when service and treatment varied according to the area one lived in; and people were afraid to go to the doctor because of the cost.

Any attempt to promote the privatisation of the health service and to see the private sector as the major provider of health care is an attempt to erode the right of people, which has been secure for 30 years, to state-provided health care.

4. Gas and Electricity Shops

Steve Lord
(NALGO Research Section)

Introduction

This section looks at the current threat to the retailing activities of two major nationalised industries — the gas and electricity industries. Both industries have a network of shops or showrooms with three main functions:

i. payment point for gas and electricity bills;
ii. enquiry points where consumers can apply for supply, ask about tariffs, arrange for servicing and repair of appliances, obtain general information on appliances and energy conservation, and raise complaints;
iii. retail outlets for appliances.

They therefore serve a range of functions unlike other retail or service operators. It is the sale of appliances which has been the subject of recent investigations, threatening the entire network of shops.

The threat to gas and electricity shops must be viewed against the background of the present Tory Government's attack on these two major energy industries and as part of the wider campaign against public industries and enterprises. On the production side, the Oil and Gas (Enterprise) Act will weaken the British Gas Corporation's (BGC) market position by enforcing the sale of its oil assets and opening up the supply of gas to private interests, whilst in the electricity case Nigel Lawson, Secretary of State for Energy, has announced that the Government intends to introduce legislation to allow private generation and sale of electricity as a main business. Taken together, the proposed measures on both production and retailing activities constitute a determined attempt by the Government to dismantle two efficient and integrated industries in order to further the interests of private profitability.

There are a number of reasons why this proposed privatisation of gas and electricity shops is of general concern and why it must be vigorously challenged:

— it is an important part of the current ideological onslaught on the concept of public enterprise and provision;

— it would put at risk at least 50,000 jobs directly, with potentially considerable secondary effects on employment;

— consumers of gas and electricity would be faced with a deterioration in standards of choice, service and safety;

— in the longer term there would be serious implications for energy conservation and the development of a coherent, planned energy policy.

Historical background

To understand the current retailing and servicing activities of the gas and electricity industries it is necessary to examine briefly their historical development. Prior to nationalisation in the second half of the 1940s, both industries were composed of several hundred undertakings (in the gas case over one thousand), run either as independent companies or by local authorities. In both industries the supply, installation and servicing of appliances, as well as the provision of information and advice, was considered as a necessary and integral part of the business of supplying gas or electricity. For example, concern about safety led many of the gas undertakings to establish service centres to sell approved appliances and ensure safe installation and servicing in the home, as a way of overcoming fears and increasing the domestic demand for gas.

In the electricity industry, undertakings were anxious to increase demand for electricity, particularly among domestic consumers and at times which would balance the industrial load. Also many local authority undertakings had a commitment to extend electricity use among low-income consumers in order to raise living standards. This led initially to hiring out electrical cookers as the purchase price represented a considerable outlay to most low-income consumers. The sale of electrical appliances increased steadily during the 1930s and these existing service and hire centres run by electricity undertakings were in a good position to meet part of this growth in demand.

At the time of nationalisation it was accepted that the existing shops and service centres were an essential element of both industries and would form an integral part of the operations of the new nationalised boards. During the 1950s and 1960s the networks of shops were rationalised by closing uneconomic outlets and opening new ones in areas of greater demand. There were also changes in the emphasis of function of the outlets, reflected by the diversity of names used — for example, shops, showrooms and service centres. By the end of the 1970s both industries had roughly the same number of shops — about 950 electricity and 930 gas shops.

An important difference revealed in the development of the appliance retailing activities of the two industries, particularly in the post-nationalisation period, is the extent of competition from private sector retailers. During the 1950s and 1960s, until the development of North Sea gas made gas increasingly competitive compared with other fuels, little interest was shown by private interests in the sale of gas appliances apart from central heating systems. Without the sustained marketing effort of the gas boards the British gas appliance manufacturing industry would have all but collapsed. It is therefore not surprising that BGC came to dominate the retailing of most gas appliances — 90 per cent of cookers, 85-95 per cent of space heaters and 65-70 per cent of water heaters, but only about 25 per cent of central heating boilers. The electrical appliance industry, by contrast, has been dominated by private sector retailers who have continually complained about the trading activities of electricity boards. These complaints have led to a number of investigations. For example, the Herbert Committee which reported in 1956 concluded:

> "We have carefully considered the objections of the trading organisations of the statutory powers accorded to the Electricity Boards against the background of the Boards' practices and policies. We find on balance that the incursion of the Electricity Boards into the retail field is in the best interests of electricity consumers who undoubtedly benefit from competition between the Electricity Board and private traders and contractors". (para.463).

A report from the House of Commons Select Committee on the Nationalised Industries in 1963 came to a similar conclusion, emphasising the importance of the retailing side of electricity boards for monitoring and influencing demand to achieve a balanced load. This explains why, during the 1970s, electricity boards came to have a relatively large share of the cooker and storage heater market, whilst private retailers dominated the market in the sale of other, often more profitable, electrical goods. Both these appliances were promoted to improve the utilisation of generating plant and hence lower the average unit price of electricity, benefiting all consumers.

During the run up to the 1979 general election the concept of privatisation figured quite prominently in the Conservative campaign, though neither the 1977 policy document "The Right Approach to the Economy" nor the Election Manifesto contained any specific reference to the gas and electricity industries. It is only in the last two years that firstly gas and more recently electricity showrooms have come under threat.

The Monopolies Commission report on domestic gas appliances

The challenge to the appliance retailing activities of the British Gas Corporation stems from the publication of a Monopolies and Mergers Commission (MCC) report in July 1980. The MCC investigation, initiated in 1977, concerned the possible existence of a monopoly situation in relation to the supply of gas cookers, space heaters and instantaneous water heaters. It therefore looked not only at the trading position of the Gas Corporation but also at the practices of the appliance manufacturers. The reference to the MCC followed a campaign mounted by several discount warehouse companies and private retailers who complained that they could not buy the appliances they wanted because BGC orders were given preference, and that the appliance manufacturers gave BGC preferential discount terms.

There was little argument that the Gas Corporation held a monopoly in the supply of the reference goods as the Fair Trading Act 1973 defines a monopoly as a situation where more than 25 per cent of a particular good is manufactured or supplied by one organisation. As was pointed out in a previous section, BGC accounts for a much higher proportion of total sales of all three reference goods. The Commission also concluded that two manufacturers, Thorn Gas Appliances Ltd and Chaffoteaux Ltd held monopoly positions, and that groups of manufacturers had acted together to restrict competition, amounting to what is called a complex monopoly. The second stage of the Commission's enquiry then considered whether these monopoly situations had acted

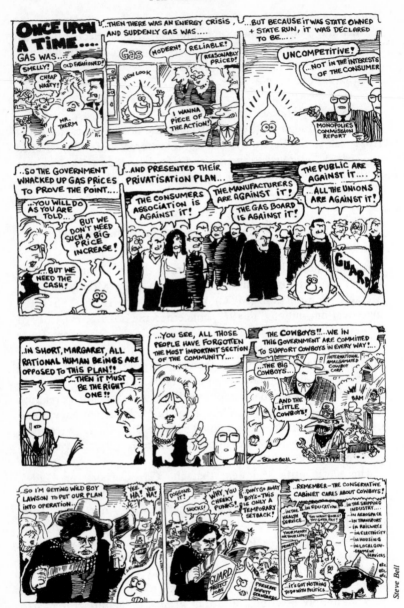

From Public Service, *January, 1982.*

against the public interest.

The Commission's report, published on 29th July 1980, concluded that the British Gas Corporation's monopoly had operated against the public interest. It argued that BGCs dominant position had had a damaging effect on appliance manufacturers, whose record of innovation, investment and exports was considered to be poor, and had limited consumer choice in the range of appliances and outlets. The aggressive sales techniques of the Corporation, particularly the SUPERFLAME scheme, and internal accounting procedures had resulted in unfair competition, damaging private sector retailers. The Commission also concluded that the monopoly exercised by Thorns and the associations had operated against the public interest, though this was seen as being due to the dominant position of BGC so no separate recommendations were made.

The Commission rather reduced the force of its arguments against BGC by admitting that if the number of showrooms was reduced there could be a loss of benefit to the public as a result of lower levels of service. It accepted that the Corporation offers specialist advice on gas conservation, which is unlikely to be given by private sector retailers, has a well trained staff, and carries a very large supply of spares. The report also conceded that the situation had improved since the reference had been made, since many of the practices originally complained of had ceased. Even while the report was being prepared there had been new entrants into the retail sector, the Corporation had given its regions more independence in their dealings with manufacturers, and investment levels had improved.

The Commission set out what it considered to be two possible courses of action:

i. that the British Gas Corporation cease trading over a three-year period so that the sale of gas appliances becomes an exclusively private sector activity; or

ii. that the Corporation's accounting and other procedures are modified in order to reduce its power in the retailing sector and its influence over manufacturers. All costs arising from the sale of appliances would have to be met from the appliance retailing account and BGC would refrain from exclusive selling deals like the SUPERFLAME scheme.

The Commission as a whole did not decide between these two alternatives. On the one hand it accepted that it could not wholly predict the result of a complete ban on BGC appliance sales. On the other, the alternative of changing the accounting procedures might not be sufficient to produce a "fully competitive retail market". The Commission concluded that the choice between the two options depended on "political considerations" and left it to the Government.

Two members of the Commission, Mr G. Ashford and Ms R. Stephen, wrote notes of preference opposing any immediate ban on the sale of gas appliances by BGC. Mr Ashford wanted the less radical solution to be introduced for a trial period of three years, whilst Ms Stephen argued that a ban would have very damaging effects on appliance manufacturers and domestic consumers.

The publication of the report was welcomed by the then Minister for Consumer Affairs, Sally Oppenheim, who indicated that the Government would examine its conclusions with a view to taking appropriate measures. However, the report was also widely criticised. The "radical" option of forcing BGC to end its appliance retailing activities was generally seen as another example of privatisation: one in which the public sector is forced to close down its operations in order to provide a new market for private sector interests. The following section summarises the arguments used by the trade unions in the gas industry to fight this threat of privatisation.

The trade union case

The trade unions in the gas industry have played a very active role in all stages of the MMC investigation and in the subsequent debate over its recommendations.. Through the TUC, both written and oral evidence was presented to the Commission emphasising the trade unions' complete opposition to any attempt to reduce BGC's activities in order to further the interests of private retailers. On publication of the report, the eight gas unions — ACTSS, ASTMS, AUEW, DSEU, GMWU, MATSA, NALGO and TASS — represented on the trade union side of the Planning Liaison Committee formed a co-ordinating body GUARD (Gas Unions Against the Report for Dismantling the BGC). This organised joint activities and produced joint publicity material outlining trade union arguments against the privatisation of gas appliance retailing.

A major concern to trade unions within the gas industry has been that the Government would use the Commission's report in furtherance of its wide attack on public sector activities and jobs. The deliberate creation of unemployment and the undermining of public enterprise and provision are essential components of the Government's monetarist economic strategy. It was therefore feared that any decision on the gas showrooms would be made on the grounds of political dogma rather than any appreciation of the real interests of gas consumers and workers.

In particular, trade unions feared that ending BGC's retailing activities would lead to the loss of a large number of jobs. Though the Commission accepted that some jobs would be lost and the quality of others reduced, it did not attempt any assessment of numbers of likely redundancies. It hoped optimistically that private enterprise would mop up some of the "surplus" manpower which would result from a ban on BGC. The unions expressed surprise and dismay that the Commission had not attempted to draw up a balance sheet of jobs lost and theoretically gained in its deliberations on the public interest. The unions argued that a more rigorous assessment would have demonstrated that the Commission's so-called "radical" proposal would have a very damaging effect on employment, both in BGC and in the appliance manufacturing industry. Trade union estimates suggested that between 25,000 and 30,000 jobs could be lost.

Sales staff and showroom assistance would be the first to suffer if BGC had to end its retailing operations. There would be a corresponding loss of jobs in accounts departments and administration. The closure of showrooms would cut both installation work and servicing, with wide implications for all BGC employers. There would also be serious effects on employment in appliance manufacturing. The Commission's main argument is that a ban on BGC would enable private retailers to expand their sales to fill the gap. This, however, would be unlikely to occur. Doubts about it have been expressed by appliance manufacturers and by at least one major discount warehouse. As union evidence to the Commission made clear, private shops and discount stores prefer to sell electrical appliances which can be sold off the shelf without follow-up work, rather than sell gas appliances which have to be supported with a skilled installation service. The likely outcome of a ban of BGC sales would be a sharp fall in demand for gas appliances and consequent reductions in employment in the appliance industry. This would also have an adverse effect on the balance of trade as British-made cookers and heaters would be replaced in the shops by foreign-made electrical goods.

Through GUARD, trade unions argued forcefully that the domestic consumer would suffer seriously if BGC was compelled to end the retailing of appliances. The Commission acknowledged that a ban on BGC retailing would lead to showrooms closing, which in many towns would not be replaced by any private sector retailer, so that, in the words of the report: ". . . such towns would lose by the closing of their local gas showroom both in its advice centre function and the wide range of stock it held, without any evident off-setting benefit". Not only would consumers lose out through the reduction in the number of appliance retailers, it is very unlikely that high street shops and discount houses would carry the same range of products as BGC, and certainly not the 2½m spares for appliances currently stocked by the Gas Corporation. Neither would there be any off-setting price reductions for consumers. The Commission could find no evidence that the BGC's dominant position had caused price rises — in fact, there are several suggestions that the corporation's monopoly might have had the effect of reducing appliance prices to the domestic consumer. The consumer would therefore be faced, in the event of the privatisation of appliance sales, with a narrower range of products available from a smaller number of outlets, possibly at higher prices.

Both the gas unions and the Corporation argued forcefully that standards of gas installation work would fall if sales passed from the BGC to private retailers, with a consequent threat to safety. The Gas Corporation has an enviable record on safety which is unlikely to be matched by the private sector. Recent statistics, for example, show that BGC installations are 15 times safer than those carried out by the private sector. In 1979 there were 151 explosions in homes due to faulty workmanship of which 146 were in installations fixed by private operators. The Commission optimistically believed that CORGI — an association of independent installers — could be expanded and their training facilities increased. However past experience gives no encouragement for this view and gas unions are concerned that safety standards would inevitably fall if the BGC is replaced by private sector installers.

In their evidence to the Commission and to the Government the unions emphasised the importance of BGC being an integrated organisation concerned with the supply of gas at one end and its usage at the other. It has therefore been able to develop work practices, methods and techniques which have conferred on the Corporation benefits of economies of scale. If the BGC is forced out of retailing it would seriously hinder the installation and servicing function. This in turn would adversely affect general maintenance work as installation provides a workforce which can be switched to maintenance if the need arises. Without this buffer of additional staff the cost of maintaining a safe network would necessarily rise. The showrooms also provide a site for general enquiries, advice and complaints on appliances, installation and servicing which can be fed back into the Corporation, affecting decisions on such matters as supply and tariffs. Without a point at which consumers can easily pay their bills defaulting might well increase with the attendant problems of disconnections. The privatisation of appliance retailing and the closure of showrooms would thus threaten the efficiency and integrity of the whole of the Gas Corporation.

In their analysis of the MMC report and the implications of a forced withdrawal by BGC from appliance sales the gas trade unions therefore concluded that there would be disastrous consequences for all gas industry employees and consumers. Jobs would be lost, consumer choice weakened and safety standards lowered in order to bolster the profitability of a small number of private sector retailers. In the debate following the appearance of the MMC report these arguments were widely publicised by the gas unions.

The Government response to the MMC report

The gas trade unions were not alone in pointing out the weakness in analysis in the MMC report. The Gas Corporation itself, consumer groups such as the Consumers' Association and the National Gas Users' Council, and the appliance manufacturers all opposed vigoriously the option of ending BGCs participation in the sale of appliances. However, the arguments used fell on deaf ears in the Government. On 8th July 1981, almost a year after the MMC report was published, Mrs Sally Oppenheim announced the Government's response.

The Government accepted the "radical" option in the report and decided that BGC should withdraw from the retailing of appliances and dispose of all showrooms over a five-year period. This went beyond the Commission's report which talked only about the ending of appliance sales and not about the compulsory disposal of showrooms. A timetable was established for the disposal of showrooms — half were to go in two years, a further quarter in the following year and the remaining quarter in the final two years.

Legislation would be introduced to enforce this decision. The Government hoped that the Gas Corporation would maintain some consumer contact points though no indication was given of what form these would take or how many there would be.

The Government's decision created a storm of opposition. The gas unions immediately called for a one-day strike on 13th July 1981 to show the strength of feeling within the Corporation's workforce. Large amounts of publicity material were produced by GUARD and a widespread publicity campaign was initiated. Public meetings were held, MPs were lobbied and the views of the gas unions were forcefully put over wherever possible. The Gas Corporation and consumer interests also argued strongly against the Government's decision, particularly emphasising worries about safety if the private sector took over a large proportion of gas appliance installations.

By the autumn of 1981 the Government had been forced to concede that they could not proceed as fast as they would like. Secretary of State for Energy, Nigel Lawson, announced in October 1981 that the safety aspects of the proposed privatisation would require complex legislation for which there would not be time in the 1981-82 parliamentary session. The Government did however introduce the Oil and Gas (Enterprise) Bill in the winter of 1981 which gave the Secretary of State wide discretionary powers to order BGC to dispose of any part of the Corporation. The Bill received the Royal Assent in the summer of 1982 so that the Government now has the power to force BGC to dispose of the showrooms. As of October 1982 there has been no announcement of Government intentions about the safety legislation required, though there is a strong possibility that some safety measures will be included in the Queen's Speech outlining legislation to be introduced in the 1982-83 parliamentary session. The Government therefore has been forced to postpone for the time being its plans for the showrooms and appears uncertain about how to tackle the safety issue. But, privatisation still remains as a major threat to the continued existence of BGC's appliance sales, and gas unions are preparing themselves for an intensification of the struggle to fight privatisation and save the gas showrooms.

The Office of Fair Trading report on the London Electricity Board

Electricity Board shops face a similar privatisation threat to that posed to gas showrooms. In both cases the impetus has come from an anti-monopoly report. In June 1981 the Director General of the Office of Fair Trading (OFT) announced that he proposed to carry out an investigation under section 3 of the Competition Act 1980 with the intention of establishing whether the London Electricity Board (LEB) had been pursuing an anti-competitive practice. The specific matters to be investigated were:

i. whether the LEB had been carrying on at a loss its business of retailing domestic electrical goods, spare parts and ancillary goods;

ii. if this was the case, whether this course of conduct had had the effect of restricting, distorting or preventing competition in connection with the production, supply or acquisition of goods.

The report, published in April 1982, contained a detailed analysis of the LEB's operations. The LEB, one of the 12 Area Boards in England and Wales, was formed in 1948 from 30 local authority electrical undertakings and 10 commercial companies. The contracting and sales of electrical appliances had a turnover of £21.8m in 1980/81, of which over £14m was derived from the sales of domestic appliances from the 57 shops within the Board's area. The report showed that the LEB overall only had a market share of around 11 per cent, but that there were variations across the main types of electrical goods. For example, the LEB accounted for only 1 per cent of sales of "brown goods" (TVs, videos and audio appliances), 7 per cent of "small appliances" (hair dryers, small kitchen appliances, shavers, etc), 13 per cent of "white goods" (fridges, washing machines), but 60 per cent of the sales of electric cookers and 60 per cent to 70 per cent of storage heaters, both of which are heavy users of electricity.

The report concluded that substantial losses had been made in the previous five years by appliance sales, though the accounting conventions adopted in the Board's published accounts understated them. For example, the OFT calculated that LEB's losses on sales were £3.5m (1980/81), £2.3m (1979/80), £2.2m (1978/79), £1.5m (1977/78) and £1.3m (1976/77). The report argued that as a result the Board was pursuing an anti-competitive practice because the Board's main business of selling electricity enabled it to continue to absorb losses in its shops, protecting them from the consequences of poor financial performance. This cross-subsidisation meant that the Board did not have the same incentive to retrench, reorganise or contract its retailing operation as private sector retailers.

The OFT admitted that the LEB cannot be described as a dominant force in its area and there was no evidence that the Board was making anti-competitive use of any monopolistic market power it might possess. For example, the Board had not used its position to undercut private retailers — figures produced by the OFT show that in 8 out of 11 months in 1981, the Board was charging higher prices than those in independent shops or multiple and discount stores. Nevertheless, the report concluded that the Board's appliance sales had been conducted in an anti-competitive manner and in June 1982 the matter was referred to the Monopolies and Mergers Commission, whose report is awaited.

The trade union case

As with gas showrooms, the trade unions in the electricity industry oppose any attempt to privatise the appliance retailing activities of electricity boards. Three unions — the EPEA, EEPTU and NALGO — have submitted joint evidence to the MMC outlining their reservations about the OFT report and stating their case for the continued participation of the LEB in appliance sales.

The central theme of the unions' evidence is that, like gas showrooms, electricity shops have objectives other than pure profitability. For example, electricity boards use their shops to serve actual and potential purchasers of electricity by providing advice, accounts and cash collection facilities and a consumer relations service, which are separable from, but complementary to, the retailing of appliances. Some 45 per cent of domestic electricity sales revenue is paid directly, particularly by the elderly and lower income groups. Withdrawal of this facility could easily alienate consumers, substantially increasing the number of bad debtors, with associated problems.

In their sales policies, the electricity boards have been concerned to develop a balanced load. They have concentrated their sales effort on appliances — particularly cookers and storage heaters — which generate a significant extra demand for electricity. The private sector, by contrast, has dominated the larger, more buoyant "brown goods" market. The boards also have a commitment to purchasing and selling largely British manufactured goods — some 90 per cent of the LEB's sales are British made appliances. This encourages investment and employment in British industries facing a high level of competition from foreign imports. It is also in the best overall interests of the Electricity Supply Industry and its consumers, because British manufacturing industries represent a significant part of electricity demand — demand which would fall if a major retailer of their products was forced to close down.

Electricity boards, including the LEB, have in addition a commitment to safety and energy conservation. Without their appliance sales, the boards would no longer be in a position to give advice on design, safety and energy efficiency to either appliance manufacturers or domestic consumers. The electricity unions therefore argue that the sale of appliances is but one function of the shops, making it unreasonable to insist that their performance and methods match those of private retailers who are concerned solely to maximise profits.

Though stressing that it is in the public interest to maintain electricity board retail outlets, the unions acknowledge that they should be as competitive as possible. The electricity unions have co-operated and will continue to co-operate in measures which will make the LEB's contracting and sales of appliances financially viable. Shop numbers have been reduced from 78 in 1951 to 55 at present; there have been recent manpower reductions and the unions are currently co-operating in a major cost reduction programme. However, it must be recognised that there are particular problems in operating in central London, an area which has a falling population of increasing average age. This has led to a competitive, declining market, not only for the LEB but for all other retailers of large electrical appliances.

It is for the reasons outlined above that the trade unions in the electricity industry believe that appliance sales have an essential contribution to make to the activities of electricity boards. Any curtailment of this function would not be in the interest of domestic consumers nor of the employees of the electricity boards and appliance manufacturers who would face large-scale redundancies. Arguments similar to those of the trade unions have been presented to the MMC by the London Electricity Board and by appliance manufacturers. However, the Commission's attitude towards the gas industry and the Government's determination to privatise large sections of the public sector do not auger well for the future of electricity boards' appliance sales.

Conclusions

- The threat of privatisation looms large over the retaililng of appliances in the gas and electricity industries. In both industries, as elsewhere in the public sector, trade unions have shown their determination to resist the onslaught on their jobs and services and fight the threat of privatisation. This section has summarised the arguments put forward by trade unions to defend gas and electricity shops. Privatisation would have a disastrous effect on jobs, both in the gas and electricity industries and in the appliance manufacturing industry. Consumers would be faced with lower levels of service, including less choice and less advice on safety and energy conservation matters. Safety standards, particularly in the gas industry, would be bound to suffer. Privatisation would make more difficult the development of a rational, planned approach to energy use. Private sector retailers respond to short-term market considerations rather than any overall assessment of longer term energy supplies and demands. In sum, two efficient and integrated organisations would be put at risk merely to benefit a handful of private appliance retailers.

- One issue to arise in both industries is the role played by the Office of Fair Trading and the Monopolies and Mergers Commission. There is considerable feeling within trade unions that these bodies are being forced to undertake political investigations of nationalised industries within narrow limits and biased against trade union interests. The TUC Nationalised Industries Committee has expressed its worries on this and has called for a meeting with trade union representatives on the MMC, but the fundamental question is raised of the continuation of trade union involvement with such bodies.

- In both cases the issue of financial procedures and particularly cross-subsidisation has been central to the debate. A major part of the argument against privatisation is that showrooms are not run simply for profit — they have other important functions such as bill payments, information on tariffs and general advice on appliances and energy conservation. However, the technical debate has been dominated by conventional capitalist accounting rather than taking into account social and non-profit objectives.

- Probably the most important lesson to emerge from the struggle against the privatisation of gas and electricity showrooms is the importance of joint union campaigns and action. Joint union initiatives at national and local level enable the threat of privatisation to be monitored more effectively; publicity campaigns and joint action can be planned more easily; and divisions between unions which weaken united opposition can be prevented.

- It is also important to consider ways of forging alliances with other interested parties. In the gas case, all the major interests — the Gas Corporation, trade unions, consumer groups and appliance manufacturers were opposed to the Government's plans. It is essential for trade unionists to discuss how the benefit of such alliances can be maximised and incorporated into joint action campaigns.

5. National Freight Corporation

Joe Irvin
(TGWU Research Department)

Introduction

"Privatisation" is a word coined by the Conservative Party to describe handing over parts of the public sector into private hands. This can take several forms including:

a. Selling off a public concern (or its subsidiary) to private owners.

b. Selling some shares in a public enterprise to private owners.

c. Withdrawing public services and allowing the private sector to provide them to the public.

d. Replacing work done by public employees with work done under contract by private companies.

The privatisation of the National Freight Corporation is a (so far) unique example of the first form of privatisation. It has been the subject of a sale to a consortium of management and employees.

This paper sets out to explain the background to the sale, the mechanics of the sale, the reasons why the TGWU opposed the sale, and the problems for the Labour Movement highlighted by this case.

Part I Background

i. The NFC

The National Freight Corporation was formed in 1969 under the Transport Act 1968 to bring together all the road freight transport interests that the Government had acquired over the years, including those owned by British Rail. It is the largest road haulage operator in Britain in an industry in which small

109

and medium-sized private operators abound.

It owns some 16,500 vehicles and employs some 26,000 people. However, it still only accounts for 6 to 7 per cent of "public" road haulage (i.e. road freight taken on behalf of other companies).

The major subsidiary groups of the NFC include British Road Services, National Carriers, Roadline, Pickfords, Tankfreight and Cartransport. A fuller list of subsidiaries is attached as *Appendix I*. Control of the Freightliners company was returned to British Rail in 1978.

A national asset? — The National Freight Company.

ii. **Privatisation**

In the Election Manifesto of 1979, the Tory Party committed themselves to privatise the National Freight Corporation, and subsequently expressed the intent to sell all, or virtually all, of the shares.

On 1st October 1980, under the terms of the Transport Act

1980, the Corporation was reconstituted as a limited liability company, the National Freight Company Limited. The new company took over the assets, liabilities and business of the Corporation, though it continued to be publicly owned since the shares were in the name of the Secretary of State for Transport.

The formation of a limited liability company was the first step in preparation for a Stock Market flotation.

iii. The Government's Plans Go Astray

The reason why the Government did not go ahead with a virtually open sale of shares (as they did in the cases of Amersham International, Cable and Wireless, and British Aerospace) was not a change of heart. What happened was that events turned in such a way as to make the NFC unattractive to potential buyers.

The main cause of the crisis in NFC's business was the withdrawal in late 1980 of British Rail's parcels contract with National Carriers. This contract for supplying collection - and - delivery services to British Rail for their BREPS (British Rail Express Parcels Service) business was worth £25 million a year. The decision follows BR's decision to close this business.

It is ironic that the Government's financial squeeze on British Rail contributed to the scuppering of their plan to sell NFC shares on the open market.

The loss of the BREPS contract was accompanied by a slump in parcel deliveries owing to the recession. The NFC's main "parcel companies" (National Carriers and Roadline) made a combined trading loss of £3m in 1980. (This is the loss *before* deducting central office costs, interest payments, tax and redundancy costs; and adding profit from property sales).

iv. Management Propose a "Buy Out"

At the time of this embarrassing impasse for the Government, the senior management of the NFC (led by Mr Peter Thompson, Chief Executive of the NFC) stepped in with a proposal to save the Government's face. This involved the management of the company buying the business from the Government and offering shares to all employees. NFC's management had never firmly opposed privatisation; they had wanted a sale of shares with conditions. They were nervous of the buy-out idea, but said there could be advantages of being in the private sector to avoid public sector financial constraints.

Part II The "Buy-out": The Mechanics of the Sale

In May 1981, a proposal for an employee "buy-out" was put to the Government; in October a conditional sale agreement was signed; and on 19th February 1982 the National Freight Company Limited became a wholly owned subsidiary of the National Freight Consortium p.l.c. This is a holding company owned jointly by employees and pensioners of the NFC, members of their families, and four banks.

The way the "buy-out" was performed was complicated:

i. **Preliminaries**

First of all, the senior management had to arrange support from the banks and a financial commitment from the NFC's management to buy shares.

ii. **The Consortium**

Secondly, it was decided to establish a consortium (the National Freight Consortium p.l.c.) which would be a holding company used to take over ownership of the National Freight Company.

iii. **The Price**

The purchase price of the National Company was put at £53.5m and agreed with the Secretary of State for Transport. Of course, NFC employees could not raise this sort of money themselves. The money was to come from four sources:
1. A large loan from the banks.
2. Purchase of shares by NFC management etc.
3. Purchase of shares by the banks.
4. An extra loan from Barclays Merchant Bank to fund an Employee Loan Scheme and to pay the costs of the transaction.

The basic pattern of the sale is illustrated in *Appendix II*.

iv. The Loan

The NFC management arranged for the Consortium set up to purchase NFC to borrow £51m in medium term loans from six banks. These were Barclays Bank Limited, Barclays Merchant Bank, County Bank Limited, Lloyds Bank Limited, National Westminster Bank Limited, and Williams and Glyn's Bank Limited. Barclays Bank and its merchant bank subsidiary provided £19,125,000 of this loan.

The loan would be repayable by annual instalments over a period of 10 years, beginning two years after the loan was given. The first three instalments would be £5m each, the final six would be £6m each.

Interest would be payable at a basic rate of one per cent above the London Inter-Bank Offered Rate.

A "participation fee" of £63,750 was payable to Banks.

v. Shares for Employees

In January 1982 an offer of subscription of 6,187,500 'A' Ordinary £1 shares in the National Freight Consortium plc was made on behalf of the Consortium by Barclays Merchant Bank Ltd. The sale was open not only to NFC employees, but also members of their families and NFC pensioners and their families.

For employees, family included spouse, children and grandchildren. For pensioners, family included only a spouse.

The transfer or resale of these shares can be made only:

a. on death or bankruptcy; or
b. "bona fide" between members of an employee's or pensioner's family; or
c. through the matching arrangement, through a "Share Trust" (see below).

Up to £3m of the purchase was to be financed through interest-free loans from the BMB under the Employee Loan Scheme (discussed below).

The *minimum* stake which any person may have is 100 shares costing £100. The *maximum* stake is 100,000 shares costing £100,000 for each *family*.

vi. The Share Trust and Transfers

The "Share Trust" would set a price for shares (through a firm of accountants) for sale to new employees; existing employees not holding shares; existing shareholders; all other would-be buyers (in that order of preference).

The job of the Share Trust is, on four days of each year, to allow the sale of shares between the buyers and sellers listed above so as to maintain the number of shares roughly intact. A growth of shares of no more than 2 per cent is allowed to account for new demand from employees.

No-one can be *forced* to sell or buy shares. Although this system is designed to keep shares "within the NFC family", it is clear that there is scope for other people to hold shares. In five years time, the directors propose to go over to an ordinary Stock Exchange quotation.

vii. **Employee Loan Scheme**

Up to three million of the approximately 6.2 million shares offered to employees/pensioners and their families could be bought under the Employee Loan Scheme.

This scheme was open only to full-time employees of the NFC, excluding Directors. Joint applications could be made by an employee and his/her spouse or children under 18, but not children over 18, or grandchildren.

The maximum loan is £200 per buyer.

The granting of a loan under the scheme is *entirely* at the discretion of the Directors.

The terms of the loan are as follows:

a. Repayment will be made by equal instalments, due on each wage or salary payment date, over a period of one year, deducted from wages at sources.
b. Interest will not be charged if those payments are on schedule.
c. However, if a loan becomes outstanding because:
   i. the employee leaves full-time employment with NFC;
   ii. the employee dies or becomes bankrupt; or
   iii. the employee defaults on any repayment; interest becomes due, payable monthly at *4 per cent above* the base rate of Lloyds Bank Limited. This can be deducted by the Company direct from money due to the employee.

d. For joint applications with members of an employee's family, all the joint applicants over 18 can be liable for repayment of outstanding money.

viii. Shares for the Banks

Four banks subscribed to 17.5 per cent of the total issued share capital. These took the form of 1,312,500 of 'B' Ordinary Shares. The Banks' holding as a proportion of all issued shares are:

Barclays Industrial Development Limited	8.1%
County Bank Limited (Nat West)	4.4%
Pegasus Holdings Limited (Lloyds)	3.75%
Williams and Glyn's Bank Limited	1.25%
	17.5%

Both sets of shares (A and B) have voting rights at the Annual General Meeting; and the same rights to dividends and capital. However, the 'B' shareholders have more rights than 'A' shareholders. Most notably, the Banks have a right to nominate directly one of the Board of Directors, as long as they hold 5 per cent of the issued share capital. Secondly, they have the right to veto any proposal which would effectively increase the amount of shares being issued over and above an agreed small amount to account for all new employees.

ix. Extra Loan from BMB

Barclays Merchant Bank agreed a short-term loan of up to £3m to fund the Employee Loan Scheme (see above). This is repayable on demand. Interest is charged at 1 per cent over the Barclay's Bank Limited's Base Rate.

Secondly, the bank agreed a separate short-term loan of £1m to cover the expenses of the proposed transaction. This is repayable on demand, but not later than six months after it was made.

x. Pensions

In order to meet the outstanding pension obligations for past service, the Secretary of State agreed to pay £47,300,000 out of the purchase prices of £53.5m to the Pension Trustee on behalf of the relevant NFC Pension Funds.

(Those employees formerly employed by British Rail would, however, continue to have pensions funded separately by the Government).

The NFC Directors reckoned that this was £2m short of the amount needed to meet all obligations for past credits.

A deficit of £10m on the Salaried Staff Scheme not related to past credits would have to be met by the NFC itself.

The Pension Rights of NFC employees would suffer since index-linked pensions would no longer be guaranteed, as they had been in practice while the NFC remained in public ownership.

The £47.3m payment by the Government meant that their net receipt from the sale was only £6.2m.

Part III   Why the TGWU opposed the Sale

The TGWU was the only union within the NFC to advise its members not to purchase shares.

i. Opposition to Privatisation

It should be stated that from the very beginning, the TGWU was implacably opposed to plans to privatise the NFC.

It has been an age-old policy of ours to support an integrated transport policy with a nationalised presence in the road haulage industry. We therefore enthusiastically supported the creation of the National Freight Corporation.

Conversely, we strongly opposed plans by the Thatcher Government to privatise public corporations such as the National Freight Corporation.

Government funding to the NFC between 1976 and 1981 amounted to some £87m million of public money invested in the corporation. We believe that this should be used for the public benefit, not private profit.

The 1980 TUC passed a resolution on the Nationalised Industries including the following:

> "An indefinite threat of privatisation directly undermines the contribution they can make to the regeneration of the economy, while the selling-off of these national assets will further undermine the economy, lead to a loss of public control and increase the influence of the multinationals. Congress is opposed to both the sale of shares and the hiving-off of profitable sectors of the

nationalised industries, and calls upon all workers not to purchase shares of a denationalised company, and for all industries denationalised to be taken back into public ownership without payment of compensation.''

At our own Conference in 1981, the anger of our members was apparent. The following resolution was passed *unanimously:*

> *National Freight Corporation — Denationalisation*
> "That this Conference deeply concerned at the Government's intention to sell off the state-owned sector of the road transport industry and at the enthusiastic co-operation of the senior management of the NFC in bringing about the Government's denationalisation policy by seeking from the private sector potential buyers of shares in the proposed denationalised public companies, demands that the next Labour Government have as its number one priority the re-establishment of a public sector road transport undertaking and that the people who have been engaged in the sabotage of the NFC including the chairman, vice-chairman, and chief executives, must be debarred from holding any managerial positions in the public sector.''

ii. The "Buy-Out"

Unlike some other unions within the NFC, the TGWU did not change its attitude when it was proposed that the potential buyers from the private sector would include employees of the company.

It was argued by some that since privatisation was inevitable, the "buy-out" proposal was the best option, and that it would prevent other private sector firms coming in and asset-stripping. Moreover, the shares were being offered to employees on favourable terms, since interest-free loans were available and the total purchase price was low.

iii. Why the TGWU Opposed the "Buy-Out"

a. *Privatisation was not inevitable*

The Government had faltered in its privatisation plans because of the unstable financial position of the NFC Group. The management's proposals for a "buy-out" offered the Government a way of saving face by carrying out privatisation.

b. *Renationalisation*

The policy of the TUC and Labour Party at the time was for

TGWU LORRY DRIVERS —SPECIAL

SOLD?

SOLD?

SOLD?

Over 22,000 TGWU members are employed in these companies of National Freight Company

BRS GROUP OF COMPANIES, THE ROADLINE GROUP OF COMPANIES, CARTRANSPORT, TANKFREIGHT, CONTRALI·PICKFORDS, TEMPCO INTERNATIONAL, PICKFORD

REMOVALS, PICKFORD HEAVY HAULAGE, PICKFORDS TRAVEL, CONTAINERWAY AND ROADFERRY, WASTE MANAGEMENT, NORTHERN IRELAND CARRIERS.

NOW A TORY TRANSPORT MINISTER PLANS TO SELL THE LOT — AND THE JOBS THAT GO WITH THEM

DON'T LET IT HAPPEN!

renationalisation of the NFC if it was placed in private ownership. The purchase of shares by trade union members would weaken the resolve to renationalise the NFC in the future.

c. *The employee "buy-out" would not prevent outside purchases*

It was not true than an employee "buy-out" would prevent the transfer of sales to non-employees. Already pensioners and family members can hold shares. Four banks hold 17.5 per cent of shares with special rights. Moreover, the Directors plan to go over to Stock Market Quotation in 1988. From then onwards, takeover bids and asset stripping would be likely.

d. *The Consortium was not a workers' co-operative*

The impression that the Consortium would lead to a Workers' Co-operative was false. Firstly, outside interests such as the Banks were already firmly entrenched in considerable power.

Secondly, the distribution of shares would inevitably make the management, particularly senior management, the other effective controlling force. Indeed, from the start this has been a management "buy-out" and not a workers' takeover. We discuss later the actual outcome of the share purchase.

Thirdly, the day-to-day running of the company would stay in the hands of those who had been in charge of the NFC previously. This was the same management which had run down the UK workforce from over 65,000 in 1970 to only 24,000 in 1981. The NFC has set aside £9m for redundancy costs in 1982/83. This could mean up to 6,000 redundancies.

e. *Interface with collective bargaining*

The unity of the workforce and union organisation could suffer because of worker shareholders. There could be a serious conflict of interest and a damaging division of loyalties between the minority of shareholders and other workers.

f. *The financial position of the company may be unsound*
Some doubt has been cast on the financial position of the NFC. The question has to be asked why the NFC was

offered for sale at £53.5m when its fixed assets alone were valued at about £100m in October 1981.

Together with the fact that the Government postponed a Stock Market flotation, this suggests that the NFC was not saleable on present prospects.

Secondly, the bank loans present a heavy burden of interest for the NFC to carry. The cost of interest for servicing the bank loans is estimated by the NFC to be £9.6m a year in 1980/81 values. From the second year after the takeover, the NFC would also be paying £5m and subsequently £6m a year in capital repayments for the loan.

In the second year, the burden of debt imposed by the loan will cost NFC about £14m. Other charges would make the amount of trading profit needed to break even about £24m. In order to pay a dividend equal to building society interest and retain £3.3m for investment, even assuming that no corporation tax is payable, trading profit would need to be £28m. This compares with the following record:

Table 1.

Trading Profit of NFC (£m)

	1976	1977	1978	1979	1980	1981*
Trading Profit**	2.2	11.6	19.5	19.6	13.2	17.8

* Year ending 3rd October 1981. Other years end on 31st October.

** Trading Profit before headquarters expenses; redundancy and pension and other costs; interest payments (except to Government); *plus* profit on property disposals. Also before tax and any extraordinary items.

Table 2

Estimate of Trading Profit Required by NFC 1983 (in 1981 values)

	£m
HQ expenses	3.1
Redundancy costs etc.	7.5
Leasing interest	3.4
Other interest payable	9.6
Repayment of loan	4.0
(Profit on property disposal)	(4.0)
Tax (0%)	—
Dividends (15% on share price)	1.1
Retained profit for investment	3.3
Required Trading Profit	28.0

That means that a rise in profits of nearly 60 per cent would be needed. In present trading conditions this seems unlikely.

g. *The Employee Loan Scheme*

It has been suggested that the interest free loan under the Employee Loan Scheme makes the purchase of shares very attractive. However, this scheme applied only to a minority of shareholdings. Moreover, it is totally at the discretion of the Directors. Finally, repayment must be made within 12 months by equal weekly or monthly intalments. Any default of payment is punishable by very heavy interest rates.

If an employee dies, is made redundant or leaves the company for other reasons, he/she must repay the whole loan at once, or else become subject to the punitive interest rates. Money can be deducted by the Company from money owed to the employee.

h. *Security of shareholders*

The difficulties of shareholders under the Employee Loan Scheme is discussed above. However, other shareholders may also have problems. If a shareholder ran into financial hardship (e.g. through redundancy) he/she might find it very difficult to sell shares under the Share Transfer arrangements. This would be particularly true where there was a large number of redundancies or if the NFC was not performing well financially.

i. *Threat of re-nationalisation*

Employee shareholders should be aware that current TUC and Labour Party policy is in favour of re-nationalising the NFC without compensation.

iv. **The TGWU Campaign**

The TGWU issued advice to members in the NFC *not* to purchase shares by several means. The TGWU Road Transport section's journal *The Highway* contained articles including a front-page leading article. A special broadsheet was produced. A leaflet was distributed and a letter sent to our officers and members in the NFC. The union preferred to dissuade members from share purchase, rather than take industrial action at that time, but there could well be action in the future if redundancies are threatened, at Roadline, for instance.

Part IV   Who Bought Shares?

The Directors of the NFC took large shareholdings. The largest shareholding is Mr. D.H. White: 56,000. The Chief Executive, Mr. P. Thompson, holds 40,000 shares. The seven Directors together hold 250,000 shares.

Before the share sale it was estimated that 100 senior managers could raise approximately £2.5m.

The journal *Motor Transport* has speculated that four million of the six million shares available to employees are owned by management. This may be an underestimate.

The NFC say in a notice to employees (18th February 1982) that the share sale was over-subscribed by nearly £1m. This may seem to indicate that the TGWU had failed to dissuade its members from participating in the scheme.

However, the NFC also say that there are 10,233 shareholders in the Consortium. 1,296 of those are pensioners or their spouses. Therefore, 8,937 managers, other employees and members of their families hold shares.

There are some 2,000 managers in the NFC and a total workforce of about 26,000 (including overseas).

Assuming that all the managers in NFC hold shares, that leaves 7,000 non-management employees holding shares. that means that 17,000 employees do *not* own shares. In percentage terms this is 70 per cent of the non-management workforce.

In other words *the majority of workers in the NFC did not buy shares*. The 2,000 managers have a disproportionate number of shares. They probably own a large majority of all "employee" shares. *This was a "management buy-out"*.

Part V   Questions for the Labour Movement

The takeover of the NFC by an employee "buy-out" raises a number of important and difficult questions for the Labour Movement.

i. Disintegrated transport policy

First of all, the privatisation of the NFC by whatever means is a serious blow to the public control of the transport industry taking the last part of "hire and reward" road haulage out of public ownership. In itself this would be a severe hindrance to an integrated transport policy under a future Labour Government. Matters could be made worse by the dismemberment of various subsidiaries of the NFC and the rundown of the NFC's operations in the search for profit. In the worst case, the NFC could fail to meet its obligations to the banks and much of the assets of the NFC (undervalued in the sale) would revert to the Banks.

ii. The challenge posed by sale to employees

The "buy-out" of the NFC is the largest example of an employee "buy-out" in the UK. As such, there are the normal difficult decisions facing trade unionists about the financial wisdom of the purchase, the nature of the new ownership and the conflict of interest between shareholders and employees.

In the case of the NFC, the TGWU considered that there were serious doubts about the financial benefit to individuals of purchasing NFC shares.

We have also been vindicated in warning that the new ownership would not shift power to worker-shareholders. This was not a workers' co-operative, but a management "buy-out" with the banks holding considerable power. Other private owners will gradually creep in as time goes by, with Stock Market quotation proposed after five years.

Finally, the conflict of interest is shown in wage negotiations and the threat of redundancy. So far company negotiations with unions on terms and conditions have not been affected, as both parties remained the same after the buy-out. The effect of the buy-out on employees' attitudes is still uncertain, but is unlikely to be great. The problem is the £28m trading profit to be made in 1983, a figure greater than in any previous year. So a squeeze on wage offers, and redundancies, seem inevitable — the prospectus finance provided for £9m for redundancy costs.

iii. Buying out a nationalised industry

These problems were compounded in the case of the NFC by the fact that it was a nationalised industry. This not only raised objections to private purchase by trade unionists, but also threatened the security of shareholders because of the likelihood of re-nationalisation (possibly, without compensation).

iv. Re-nationalisation and compensation

Existing TUC and Labour Party policy is that the NFC will be re-nationalised *without* compensation. However, this case in particular has brought this policy into question. Several leading trade unionists have relented at the thought of commandeering shares from trade unionists within the NFC.

As a result of this and other considerations, the TUC General Council and the Labour Party NEC are recommending to their respective Conferences a change of policy. They are recommending that compensation should be paid, but only on a "refund" basis. That means that an NFC shareholder who bought shares for £200 would get exactly £200. No account would be taken of the going market price of shares, appreciation or depreciation, or of inflation. On the other hand, no account would be taken of dividends received since the purchase of shares.

There was consideration of making more generous provision for employee shareholders and pension funds. However, no special privileges for these groups are being proposed.

Part VI Conclusion

The sale of the National Freight Corporation to private individuals partly through a sale of shares to employees raised particular problems for the trade unions involved. An alliance of consumers against the proposal was not practicable and industrial action was not thought appropriate by the unions, so the TGWU concentrated on trying to persuade members not to buy shares.

Although privatisation was opposed in principle, some unions did not oppose the purchase of shares by employees. The TGWU consistently opposed this sale mainly on these grounds:

- the financial security of employee shareholders was doubtful;
- the new firm would not be a workers' co-operative, but would leave power in the hands of management and the banks;
- there would be an inevitable conflict of interest between shareholders and employees;
- privatisation was not inveitable.

It was a matter of judgement whether the share sale was a "second best" option or whether it should be resisted.

In the event, the company remains in the control of senior management and the banks, and the majority of non-management staff did not purchase shares. The NFC buy-out also raises the problem of wider share ownership — Waste Management Ltd., which is tendering for local authority service contracts, is a subsidiary of NFC.

APPENDIX I

Subsidiary and Associated Companies

Listed below are the Subsidiaries (other than dormant Subsidiaries) of the National Freight Company Limited consolidated in the accounts. Unless otherwise stated they are wholly-owned and incorporated in Great Britain. The groupings are shown as at 3rd October 1981.

British Road Services Group

British Road Services Ltd.
    Bridges Transport Ltd.
    Eastern British Road Services Ltd.
    H.S. Morgan Transport (Southampton) Ltd.
    Midlands British Road Services Ltd.
    Morton's (BRS) Ltd.
    North Eastern British Road Services Ltd.
    North Western British Road Services Ltd.
    Southern British Road Services Ltd.
    Watsons (Carriers) Ltd.
    Western British Road Services Ltd.
    William Cooper & Sons (Carriers) Ltd.

National Carriers Group

National Carriers Ltd.
    Fashionflow Ltd.
    Fashionflow (National Carriers) Ltd.
    PBDS (National Carriers) Ltd.

Roadline UK Group

Roadline UK Ltd.
    Hanson Haulage Ltd.
    Islandlink (Jersey) Ltd. — Incorporated in Jersey.

Pickfords Group

Pickfords Industrial Ltd. (formerly Pickfords Heavy Haulage Ltd.)
Pickfords Removals Ltd.
    Howship & Company Ltd.
Pickfords Travel Service Ltd.

Special Traffics Group

Cartransport Ltd.
    Auto Freight Transport (NI) Ltd. — Incorporated in Northern Ireland.
Containerway and Roadferry Ltd.
    Ferry Trailers Ltd. — Incorporated in Northern Ireland.
Cotrali-Pickfords Ltd. (b)
    Manchester Number One Bonded Warehouse Company Ltd.
    Cotrali S.A.R.L. — Incorporated in France.
Lawther and Harvey Ltd. — Incorporated in Northern Ireland.
    Lawther and Harvey (Ireland) Ltd. —

Incorporated in the Republic of
Ireland.
Pickfords International Air Charter Co.
Ltd.
Summers the Plumbers Ltd.
Tankfreight Ltd.
  Felixstowe Tank Developments Ltd.
    (outside shareholding: 20 per cent)
Waste Management Ltd.
  Waste Clearance (Holdings) Ltd.
  Hedco Landfill Ltd.
  Norwaste Ltd. and subsidiaries.

Scottish Freight Group

Scottish Road Services Ltd. (a).
Scottish Parcel Services (b).

Tempco Group

Tempco International Ltd.
  Tempco T.I. Engineering Services Ltd.
  Gerdor Ltd. — Incorporated in the
    Republic of Ireland.
  Frigiwest (Heathrow) Ltd.

Other Companies

NFC International Holdings Ltd. (b)
National Freight Company (International)
Ltd.
NV Pickfords International SA —
Incorporated in Belgium.
Pickfords International (Holdings) France SA
— Incorporated in France (c)
Pickfords International (Nederland) BV —
Incorporated in Holland.
Pickfords International (UK) Ltd.
Freight Computer Services Ltd.
Star Bodies (NFC) Ltd.
Airlink (European) Ltd.
NFC Trading Ltd. (formerly Latham's
Coventry Ltd.)
Freight Indemnity and Guarantee Company
Ltd.

Notes:

a. Scottish Road Services Ltd., has in issue £500,000 of preference shares not held by National Freight Company Limited.

b. Cotrali-Pickford Ltd. was a Subsidiary of NFC International Holdings Ltd. It has since become a direct subsidiary of National Freight Company Limited.

c. Pickfords International (Holdings) France SA is virtually dormant, its former subsidiaries have been liquidated.

Associated Companies

Listed below are the investments in Associated Companies, which are incorporated in Great Britain unless otherwise stated.

Company and Country incorporation or registration			Total issued Capital £	Pro-portion held %	Latest Audited Accounts
Held by National Freight Company Limited:					
CL Instruments Ltd	Shares		143	30.1	31.12.80
	Loan		336,000	30.1	—
Grainhurst Properties Ltd.	Ord Shares		100	40.0	None
	Pref Shares		600	100.0	prepared
Northern Ireland Carriers Ltd. (Northern Ireland)	Shares		500,0000	50.0	31.12.80
	Loan Stock		1,500,000	50.0	—
Held by subsidiaries:					
Irish Cold Stores Ltd. (Republic of Ireland)	Shares	(Irish)	100,000	50.0	31.12.81
	Loan	(Irish)	1,000,000	50.0	—
Tempco Severnside Ltd.	Shares		2,000	49.9	27.6.81
	Loan		1,676,429	64.1	—
Tidiways Ltd	Shares		10,000	50.0	31.12.80
Vincent-Cottell Ltd.	Shares		6,000	40.0	30.9.81

APPENDIX II

How the Purchase was Financed

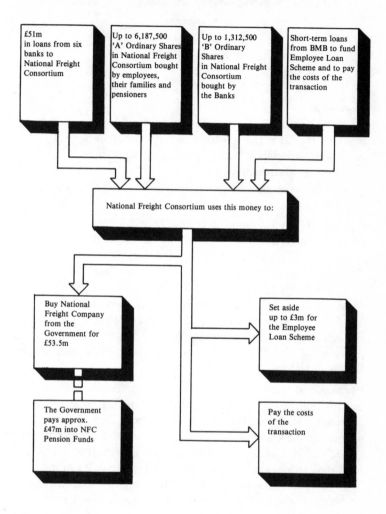

£51m
in loans from six
banks to
National Freight
Consortium

Up to 6,187,500
'A' Ordinary Shares
in National Freight
Consortium bought
by employees,
their families and
pensioners

Up to 1,312,500
'B' Ordinary
Shares
in National Freight
Consortium
bought by
the Banks

Short-term loans
from BMB to fund
Employee Loan
Scheme and to pay
the costs of the
transaction

National Freight Consortium uses this money to:

Buy National
Freight Company
from the
Government for
£53.5m

Set aside
up to £3m for
the Employee
Loan Scheme

The Government
pays approx.
£47m into NFC
Pension Funds

Pay the costs
of the
transaction

6. British Telecom

Chris Bulford

(POEU Research Department)

Background

Since 1979, British Telecom (BT) has suffered from privatisation principally through the creation of private competition. The Government has shown continuing interest and there has been a series of policy statements.

The *1981 Telecommunications Act,* which was a centre-piece of Tory legislation:

1. Ended BT's monopoly over the provision of a national telecommunications network. It was not originally intended to create a rival network, but the Government set up a study under Professor Beesley and used its lightweight and very biassed report to justify the case for a 'competitive environment'. Hence *Project Mercury,* which is backed by Cable and Wireless, BP and Barclays Merchant Bank, and which is aimed exclusively at the lucrative business market. *Project Mercury* also raised the problem of differing union interests, as some unions in the supply industries are in favour.

2. "Liberalised" the supply of *terminal equipment,* so that, subject to constraints about standards, virtually anyone can now supply equipment to put at the end of a telephone line after the first telephone. BT and its UK suppliers were probably rather slow to develop and install equipment, allowing business users and importers to persuade the Government to break its monopoly. The 1981 Act allowed a much freer regime, but there are problems over standards and safety, since a new network of regulations is required now that BT has ceased to be the standard setter. BT has been accused of acting slowly over the new regulations, which have been developed by the British Standards Institute, for example, but these inevitably take time to get right.

3. Enabled BT's telephone lines to be used for competitive services,

commonly called *value added services;* for instance, data processing and storage, answering facilities, where BT previously had a monopoly.

4. Gave the Secretary of State wide powers to *sell off* nominated *subsidiary companies* of BT. This provision of the 1981 Act has in fact been overtaken by the White Paper proposing the privatisation of the whole of BT.

Post Office

System X will revolutionise Britain's telephone system; who will control the revolution?

The White Paper, "The Future of Telecommunications in Britain"

According to the Secretary of State for Industry in his statement on the White Paper on Monday 19th July 1982, the Government will introduce a Bill in the autumn of 1982 which will enable them to turn BT into a private company under the 1948 Companies Act. If successful the Bill will become law in the spring/summer 1983.

However, the actual sale of shares has been postponed until after the next General Election. If they win that, the next Tory Government will then sell off 50 per cent + 1 shares in BT plc. Because of the scale of the operation — it would be by far the largest ever sale of shares in the UK — it is unlikely that this will happen all at once and will probably take place in two or three blocks of shares.

The justification used by the Government for its privatisation proposal is that it will release BT from the constraints of the Public Sector Borrowing Requirement (PSBR). However, it is also clear that they are intent on using privatisation as a means of "increasing efficiency" in BT via a greater concentration of profitable services and by job reductions etc.

Of direct interest to employees is the Government's intention to cover some of the existing BT pension fund deficit and other liabilities. It is not clear, however, whether this merely means past service or also includes future service. This could be a major complicating factor for the Government, because the BT scheme is fully funded and index linked. In addition, the Government will certainly offer heavily discounted shares to employees in an effort to buy off the staff.

The consequences for BT's consumers

The consequence of the liberalisation and other measures implemented so far is that the concept of a national integrated telecommunications network, open to all irrespective of geographical location or type of user, has ended. This is because the Government has insisted that in order to compete against the new rivals which the liberalisation programme has created, BT cannot cross-subsidise its operations. Every operation must be at arm's length and fully costed. This, together with the very ambitious financial targets set by Government, means that BT will inevitably have to run down and eliminate services which are not profitable or which achieve less than average profitability. Alternatively the prices of these services will have to be forced up, which, in practice, will price them out of the reach of many customers and which in turn will make them uneconomic. Obviously the services most at risk are those which provide some element of community service, for example:

1. Residential customers are now expected to pay virtually the same charges as business customers, despite the fact that the latter claim them as tax deductible expenses. This imposition on the domestic consumer is called 'rebalancing the tariffs'.

    As the POEU's evidence to the Department of Industry on the White Paper says:

    "A degree of cross-subsidisation of residential customers by business customers is desirable if we are to promote the maximum penetration of telephone service throughout the nation. However, the detrimental effect of competition on the residential customer has already been seen with recent tariff increases being twice the level of those for business customers. Privatisation will accentuate this 're-balancing' process".

2. The residential connection charge is now only £10 below that for the business customer and at £75 is clearly beyond most of the 25 per cent of homes currently without a telephone. There is a real danger of two nations developing; those with and those without a telephone. This is socially divisive in the age of information technology. However, eliminating cross-subsidisation will particularly hit rural Tory voters, and this situation could be exploited.

3. Loss of rural services, expecially a reduction in the number of public telephone kiosks.

At the same time as these effects on services are taking place, BT is being forced to compete in the most lucrative markets where, naturally, competitors are seeking to cream off the profits. This is reducing BT's profitability overall and will make it more difficult to support less than average profitable services, if this was desired.

As a public corporation, BT is required to operate a national service for the community as a whole. It is publicly accountable through Parliament for this. Customers have statutory rights to monitor it. Privatisation will end this public service duty and lead to a reduction in service. On the evidence to date, the privatisation will mean a direct threat to the jobs of POEU members in BT.

The commercialisation of BT is also leading to very important changes in the corporation's procurement policy. It is beginning to look for equipment on a worldwide basis rather than just in the UK where, currently, BT makes 95 per cent of its purchases. Since over 70 per cent of the output of British telecommunications manufacturers goes to BT, there are very serious job implications for the 100,000 employees in the industry.

People in rural areas may not see him again.

The union response

The POEU put a great deal of its effort against the 1981 Act into a Parliamentary campaign. But the new measures are fundamental and a major inter-BT union campaign of opposition to privatisation will be launched.

The Government justifies privatisation on the grounds of BT's difficulties in getting investment finance. The union wants more financial flexibility, for example external loan finance and Busby Bonds, but the Government's solution, because of its doctrinaire definition of PSBR, is privatisation. If privatisation provides free shares to all employees along the lines of British Aerospace, where 90 per cent of employees took up such an offer, this could be a difficult issue to handle.

The union also faces the problem of how to maintain a continuous campaign when the Government keeps shifting its case and strategy. The POEU will use industrial action when there is a direct threat to jobs and members are motivated. There is the problem of when to take action as privatisation will take three or four years.

All BT unions are opposed to privatisation, but some in the supplying companies are in favour. The BT unions have tried to convince them that privatisation means that imports will increase.

The union has made an extensive study of the position in the USA and found that the big telecoms corporations there, such as AT&T, have the same sort of problems as BT.

The questions privatisation raises

● Against an ideological Government, committed to privatisation, opposition must be broad-based.

● The Government is continuously pressing privatisation; it is difficult to agree anything with Government which holds for more than a few weeks. The BT Act allows the Secretary of State very wide powers to increase competition at a stroke of the pen.

● Privatisation cannot be divorced from the general issue of the purpose and the role of public corporations. As currently structured, are they out-moded? Has the labour movement been too conservative in its attitude to nationalised industry financing? The definition of the public sector borrowing requirement, which includes nationalised industry net external borrowing, is the Achilles heel of a nationalised industry wanting to invest heavily in a relatively short space of time.

BT's current difficulties starkly raise the question of how well the big public corporations are suited for the 1980s. If the Labour Government had redefined the PSBR, the problem would have been different. BT has been forced by external financing limits into a spiral of increasing tariffs in order to sustain its huge investment programme. The union has adopted

a policy of financial flexibility for nationalised industries and this must be implemented by the next Labour Government. Government control is also a key issue since the investment cut-backs ordered by the Government in the mid-70s seriously damaged the Corporation, and the effect of this is still very important today, several years later.

- The most damning problem facing those opposing privatisation is the public's belief that nationalised industries are often inefficient. The public want reassurance that the public corporations are run effectively.

- Privatisation has been used as a means of attacking the working conditions of those in the public sector. However, the ordinary trade union member's response to this has been significantly influenced by the immediate post-1979 political situation, i.e., the fact that the election of a very right-wing Government reflected a general move away from the 'corporate state' and the obvious difficulties the Labour movement has been having in adjusting to the new environment and to the defeat of the Labour Government in 1979.

7. The Construction Industry

Judith Secker
(Union of Construction, Allied Trades and Technicians (UCATT) Research
Department)

In contrast to other industries which are threatened with
privatisation, the construction industry is already largely a
privately owned industry. Only one quarter of all workers in the
construction industry (including white collar workers) work for the
public authorities (gas, water, electricity supply, NHS, Civil Service
and Local Authorities). The Local Authorities are by far the
biggest employer of construction workers in the public sector.
Seventy thousand manual workers are covered by UCATT's Local
Authority Agreement.

It is worth contrasting the private and public sectors of the
industry in five key areas before going on to study the effect of
Tory policies, their plans for the future and the trade union
response.

Job Security

Public sector empoyees on the whole have guaranteed long term
employment with the consequential protection of legal employment
rights. In the private sector workers are taken on on a casual basis,
for the duration of a site at most. Main contractors are increasingly
cutting back on directly employed workers and are replacing them
by using sub-contractors, who hire their labour for the job, often
on a self-employed basis. In 1981 alone, the top ten construction
companies cut their workforce by over 15 per cent (see Appendix
A).

As a result few workers in the private sector will have been
employed by one employer for long enough to enjoy normal
employment rights.

Employment Conditions

In the public sector paid holidays, sick pay and pensions are
entitlements which compare well with similar benefits in other

138

industries. In the private sector these benefits have only recently been won and are still well below the standard set by other industries. In particular, the Holidays with Pay Scheme works on a stamp credit system hedged with a penalty clause which is notorious in the industry where it is used by some employers to avoid making payments. And the death benefit and lump sum retirement benefit are dependent on the accrual of stamps. Lump workers will sell these hard won rights; and every month the Holidays with Pay company supplies the union with a long list of firms who are not operating the scheme.

Equal opportunities for women are unheard of in the private industry, while one or two local authorities are making progress in this direction. Above all the blacklisting of union activists which is a central feature of the private industry is not present in Local Authorities.

Health and Safety

Working in the construction industry is notoriously dangerous. In 1980 there was a total of 151 deaths in the construction industry compared with a total of 136 for the whole of the manufacturing industry. Reported non-fatal accident figures are rising despite the decline in employment in the industry. The hazards are numerous. The risks of working at height are well known. Less well known are the risks of working with dangerous chemicals on sites. And all these risks are increased when workers are employed on a casual basis, when speed rather than safety becomes the priority. Local Authorities have been far more concerned with the implementation of the Health and Safety at Work Act than private contractors. The Direct Labour Organisations (DLOs) and the nationalised industries together employ over 20 per cent of the country's construction workforce. But they have just 10 per cent of the fatal accidents in the industry — a clear indication of the higher priority which they accord to safety. A further indicator is the fact that the vast majority of safety representatives attending union training courses are from the public sector — since public sector employers have adopted a more positive attitude towards safety at work and towards union organisations.

Training

Local Authority DLO's have maintained a steady commitment to

The public sector has provided rare training opportunities for women in construction work.

training for the industry. In 1977 they employed 23 per cent of all operatives but were responsible for training 46 per cent of apprentices and trainees. In some areas courses at local colleges are only kept going by the supply of apprentices from the local authority. In Sandwell, for example, 50 per cent of carpenter apprentices, 65 per cent of bricklayers and 65 per cent of painters on courses are employed by the local authority.

Trade union organisation

The attack on DLO's is also an attack on trade union organisation. Local authority workers are the backbone of UCATT organisation and finance. They do not on the whole experience the same problems as their private sector colleagues in getting paid and unpaid time off work to carry out union duties and to get involved in trade union activity. As a result a high proportion of UCATT Branch Secretaries and Regional representatives are public sector workers. Relative security of employment in the public sector also means that the contributions made by DLO construction workers are a stable source of union finance.

The indirect Tory attack

Increasing privatisation of the construction industry is being brought about by indirect as well as direct attacks. Public sector cuts, 'cash limits', council house sales and a building moratorium have all taken their toll since the 1979 General Election. Appendix B shows output by all contractors, including public sector direct works departments from 1970 to 1981.

Since 1979 output has clearly declined in both sectors, but the public sector has been drastically reduced. In 1979 public sector non-housing work accounted for 44.08 per cent of all non-housing work. By 1981 this figure had dropped to 41.86 per cent.

The most drastic change has occurred in public sector housing. In 1979 public sector housing accounted for 41.7 per cent of all new housing. In 1981 public sector housing accounted for only 34.81 per cent of new housing.

The direct Tory attack

Since April 1981, when the Local Government Planning and Land Act came into force, the attack has been a direct one. DLO's are required to be competitive and profitable. They have to tender against private contractors for all but the smallest of projects and show a rate of 5 per cent return on capital employed for each separate project.

The Tories claim to be making DLO's compete fairly. But DLO's, unlike private contractors, cannot tender in the private sector. Private contractors do not have to publish detailed accounts on each job done and are free to cross- subsidise from one job to another. The real aim of course is to eliminate Direct Labour Organisations, which building employers have traditionally seen as the basis for a future nationalised industry. Alterations were made to the Act in its progress through Parliament directly in line with the lobbying of construction employers' organisations. For exactly the same reason they have actively and successfully lobbied for a harder line in the 1982 Employment Act which amongst its other attacks will reinforce the effects of the Local Government Planning and Land Act by penalising authorities which attempt to insist on union-only labour on their building sites.

The union response

UCATT has fought back at all levels of the union's organisation against the Tory attempt to privatise the industry. At national level the union's pamphlet *Defend Direct Labour* has been widely circulated and published. A Model Agreement has been prepared for the union's negotiators in local authorities, and with minor changes for Health Service negotiators. The Agreement provides for:

● As much building and civil engineering work as possible to be awarded to the Authority's directly employed labour force.

● Union representatives to inspect the Authority's approved list of contractors.

● The Authority to approve contractors' safety policies and to require a written undertaking on Health and Safety.

● Contractors to prove that they employ the same ratio of apprentices to craftsmen as the Authority.

● Contractors to satisfy the Authority and the Union that they are properly registered with the National Joint Council for the Building Industry.

● Contractors to satisfy the Authority and the Union that their operatives are registered with the Holidays with Pay Stamp Scheme and that stamps are being purchased.

● All operatives used on a Local Authority Contract to be directly employed.

● The removal of contractors out of compliance with the agreement from the Authority's approved list.

The response in the Regions has been extremely effective. No Tory Council has yet been able to close a Direct Works Department and a number of local authorities have already signed the Model Agreement. Where necessary the union's policies have been policed by industrial action, lobbies and mass meeetings. These policies have been strongly reaffirmed by the 1982 National Delegate Conference.

APPENDIX A

Workforce Trimmed by Slump

(from *Construction News,* 8 July 1982)

In one of the biggest falls in employment for years, the top ten construction companies shed over 15 per cent of their workforce last year (see table).

The figures, compiled from annual company reports, show that, despite other lean years, the biggest shake-out occurred in 1981. Total employment of the top ten in 1980 was 121,134, which plummeted in a single year to 108,802.

But the pattern is far from uniform. John Laing recorded the biggest drop, a fall of 16.7 per cent from 17,300 to 14,400. It was followed by George Wimpey — a 15.3 per cent drop from 26,000 to 22,000.

Others were (percentages in brackets): Tarmac, 21,739 to 18,585 (14.5); William Press, 11,800 to 10,100 (14.4); Costain, 5,427 to 4,974 (8.3); Taylor Woodrow, 10,010 to 9,512 (4.9); Balfour Beatty, 10,582 to 10,071 (4.8); John Mowlem, 6,043 to 5,786 (4.2); Bovis, 6,427 to 6,190 (3.6).

The only company to go against the trend was Sir Robert McAlpine. It actually boosted its workforce from 5,807 to 6,464, an increase of 11.3 per cent.

The employment figures for the second ten largest companies shows less of a decrease. Overall, this group suffered a drop of 13.8 per cent, with companies such as Robert M Douglas and Y J Lovell showing workforce increases.

The scale of the shedding of labour is alarming to both trade unionists and the Construction Industry Training Board. Since the mid-70s there has been a steady growth in labour-only subcontracting firms. In 1977 they provided 23.75 per cent of the total training levy collected by the training board. And this year they are expected to provide about 43 per cent.

There is a belief in some quarters that a pattern has now been established, with the directly employed workforce unlikely to increase much in the forseeable future, and that contractors will increasingly turn to labour-only gangs to carry out work.

This is a move that will disappoint the CITB which believes little training is undertaken by these firms and by unions who find it difficult to recruit in this field.

Two financial surveys by ICC bear out this picture of severe cost cutting to maintain contract work.

It says the industry, in spite of major problems, has maintained itself in remarkably good shape. Cost-cutting by construction companies to maintain profitability has forced construction workers to suffer most of all with shorter working weeks and high levels for redundancy.

And it adds: "The percentage of work in industry has forced very low tender prices in order to guarantee sufficient work, but many companies may find themselves trapped in contracts at very low prices. This could severely affect the immediate financial recovery of many smaller firms.

Employment by Top 20 Contractors 1977-81

	1981	1980	1979	1978	1977
George Wimpey	22,000 (£7,455)	26,000 (£6,731)	27,000 (£5,481)	26,000 (£4,577)	26,000 (£4,038)
Tarmac	18,585 (£6,572)	21,739 (£5,771)	23,688 (£4,812)	24,081 (£4,207)	24,019 (£3,821)
John Laing	14,400 (£6,528)	17,300 (£5,838)	18,300 (£4,918)	18,600 (£4,193)	18,900 (£3,809)
Costain Group	4,974 (£7,476)	5,427 (£6,599)	5,587 (£5,729)	5,872 (£4,978)	5,282 (£4,127)
Taylor Woodrow	9,512 (£7,149)	10,010 (£6,395)	10,062 (£5,367)	9,976 (£4,611)	10,373 (£4,068)
Balfour Beatty	10,071 (£7,756)	10,582 (£7,113)	11,042 (£5,632)	10,600 (£4,935)	10,041 (£4,537)
Bovis	6,190 (£6,878)	6,426 (£6,420)	6,364 (£5,573)	6,898 (£4,554)	7,417 (£4,252)
John Mowlem	5,786 (£6,930)	6,043 (£6,354)	6,216 (£5,599)	6,166 (£5,005)	6,220 (£4,518)
William Press Group	10,100 (£8,911)	11,800 (£7,627)	12,700 (£5,984)	12,700 (£4,882)	13,700 (£4,307)
Newarthill (Sir Robert Mcalpine)	6,464 (£6,945)	5,807 (£5,721)	5,150 (£4,896)	5,033 (£4,395)	6,073 (£4,269)
Totals for first ten companies	108,082 (£7,260)	121,134 (£6,457)	126,109 (£5,399)	125,926 (£4,634)	128,025 (£4,175)

Company					
Fairclough Construction Group	9,612 (£3,945)	9,518 (£4,410)	9,437 (£4,944)	8,543 (£5,888)	6,927 (£6,588)
Marchwiel (Sir Alfred McAlpine)	7,877 (£3,267)	6,659 (£4,956)	7,598 (£5,659)	7,463 (£6,566)	5,887 (£7,644)
French Kier Holdings	5,223 (£4,401)	4,756 (£4,406)	5,458 (£5,397)	5,045 (£6,127)	4,112 (£7,231)
Norwest Holst Holdings	4,712 (£3,345)	4,618 (£3,997)	5,556 (£4,082)	5,827 (£5,661)	5,129 (£6,769)
Y.J. Lovell (Holdings)	2,276 (£3,520)	2,226 (£4,001)	3,492 (£4,330)	3,329 (£5,568)	3,275 (£5,976)
F.J.C. Lilley	2,069 (£4,750)	2,365 (£5,649)	3,359 (£5,433)	3,474 (£5,872)	3,293 (£6,590)
Higgs and Hill	2,511 (£3,887)	2,272 (£4,397)	2,297 (£5,093)	1,975 (£5,580)	1,549 (£6,591)
London and Northern Group	7,027 (£4,162)	5,345 (£4,513)	5,567 (£5,017)	5,352 (£5,966)	4,825 (£6,618)
Robert M. Douglas (Holdings)	3,483 (£3,161)	3,322 (£3,467)	3,260 (£3,938)	3,495 (£4,486)	3,540 (£5,144)
A. Monk	4,106 (£3,811)	3,824 (£4,187)	3,779 (£4,445)	3,935 (£5,175)	3,217 (£6,294)
Totals for second ten companies	48,896 (£3,825)	44,905 (£4,398)	49,803 (£4,834)	48,438 (£5,690)	41,754 (£6,544)
Grand totals for all twenty companies	176,921 (£4,000)	170,831 (£4,516)	175,912 (£5,116)	169,572 (£6,073)	149,836 (£6,902)

The figures given are for the average weekly number of employees. The numbers employed at the year end by each company are, with few exceptions, not available.
Bracketed figures denote average annual pay.

APPENDIX B

Construction Output — Great Britain

(At 1975 Prices)

	New Housing		Other New Work			All New Work	Repair and Maintenance			All Repair and Maintenance	All Work £m
	Public	Private	Public	Private Industrial	Private Commercial		Housing	Other Work Public	Private		
1970	1,738	1,818	3,269	1,557	1,442	9,825	1,473	1,262	591	3,327	13,152
1971	1,594	2,088	3,157	1,496	1,578	9,913	1,516	1,268	568	3,352	13,265
1972	1,424	2,277	3,160	1,334	1,530	9,724	1,744	1,369	565	3,677	13,401
1973	1,387	2,375	3,085	1,218	1,563	9,629	1,956	1,327	578	3,861	13,489
1974	1,345	1,711	2,681	1,183	1,424	8,343	1,896	1,252	613	3,761	12,103
1975	1,482	1,543	2,511	1,174	1,291	8,001	1,658	1,228	531	3,417	11,418
1976	1,640	1,645	2,492	1,120	1,137	8,033	1,527	1,159	528	3,214	11,248
1977	1,491	1,557	2,379	1,298	1,136	7,860	1,589	1,163	575	3,328	11,187
1978	1,402	1,762	2,278	1,378	1,262	8,082	1,843	1,305	707	3,855	11,937
1979	1,164	1,627	2,063	1,426	1,191	7,470	1,968	1,353	721	4,041	11,511
1980	953	1,289	1,853	1,345	1,217	6,657	2,072	1,441	755	4,267	10,924
1981	604	1,131	1,682	1,058	1,278	5,752	1,850	1,316	659	3,825	9,576

Source: Housing and Construction Statistics

8. Civil Service

Andy Batkin

(Society of Civil and Public Servants (SCPS) Research Department)

This paper surveys the extent of privatisation and hiving-off (to quasi-public sector bodies) in the Civil Service at September 1982. The constraint of rigid departmental staff-in-post targets is identified as an additional motive for privatisation in the Civil Service that is absent in local authorities and nationalised industries. Examples are given of departments being prepared to increase costs through privatisation in order to achieve manpower cuts.

The approximate number of jobs (industrial and non-industrial grades) *already lost or immediately threatened* through privatisation or hiving off, is as follows:

Property Services Agency
Design	900
Supplies	540

Department of Transport
HGV Testing Stations	900

Department of Environment
District Audit Service	550
Ancient Monument and Historic Buildings	2000
Hydraulics Research Station	258
Countryside Commission	101

Ministry of Defence
Royal Ordnance Factories	19000
Claims Commission	80
Quedgeley Accommodation Stores	495
*Museums	205

Cleaners
Ministry of Defence (full-time equivalent)	4700
Inland Revenue	365

DHSS
Employers Statutory Sick Pay	3500

Ministry of Agriculture, Fisheries & Food
Cattle breeding centre, Shenfield   30
TB production and testing   15
National Collections, Tory   7
Royal Botanic Gardens Kew   527

Central Office of Information
COI Film Unit   26

Department of Energy
Gas Meter Examiners   10

Department of Industry
CAD Centre   6
National Maritime Institute   270

Royal Hospital, Chelsea   200

TOTAL   34,685

This total represents one third of the Civil Service staff cut required by April 1984.

Note: This paper only covers areas where privatisation is either decided or imminent. It does not cover areas where privatisation proposals appear to have been defeated (e.g. Ordnance Survey or Building Research Establishment) or where plans are just beginning to develop (e.g. reprographic work; cleaning — other than I.R. & MOD) or up for future consideration (e.g. Department of Employment Professional and Executive Register). PSA Estates work is included because although staff implications are not clear, privatisation studies are well advanced. Areas with Civil Service Union representation outside the Civil Service (e.g. Post Office, British Telecom) are not included.

Introduction

For local authorities and nationalised industries the motives for privatisation are two-fold. First it is the belief that private industry "should" perform as many functions as it wishes, in preference to public bodies; that the role of the public sector should be mopping up those tasks that the private sector is unwilling to take on. Second is the unproven assertion that tasks are more "efficiently" carried out in the private sector, and that in some way better value for money is obtained from private contractors in pursuit of a profit margin, than from directly employed labour chasing bonus payments.**

With its own employees, however, the Government has created a

*   Information supplied by the Institute of Professional Civil Servants (IPCS).
**   "Public or Private — The Case Against Privatisation", LRD, May 1982.

third incentive for departments to privatise and hive-off (to quasi-public sector bodies) as many functions as possible. Unlike local authorities and nationalised industries, Government departments have to meet rigid staff-in-post targets, set four years in advance.

Since 1976, cash limits have been the main instrument for achieving spending control within Government departments. Approximately 60 per cent of Government spending is cash limited. The main exception is 'demand-led' spending on unemployment and supplementary benefits, although this is not to imply that these have not been cut back in a variety of ways. Soon after the election in May 1979, however, the Cabinet changed emphasis from direct cash control to fixed manpower targets. In May 1979, an immediate recruitment freeze was imposed, resulting in a job loss of 20,000. In December, another 39,000 jobs over three years were lined up for the axe following a "cuts options" exercise by the then Lord President, Christopher Soames. In March 1980, a further cut of 15,000 was announced. These piecemeal efforts were synthesised on 13th May 1980, when the Prime Minister announced that the Government had selected a staff-in-post figure which it proposed to achieve by 1st April 1984, at the end of its five-year term. This figure of 630,000 demanded a cut in staff of 1 in 7 from the 732,000 in post in 1979. It was arrived at with something less than precision. The departmental totals for 1984 were not made available until November 1980, and it is clear that even that 6-month pause for second thoughts did not help departments save themselves from the consequences of being tied to arbitrary manpower cuts figures bearing no relation whatever to actual demand.

For many departments, achieving staff reductions on the scale demanded has proved very difficult. So-called 'efficiency' cuts — trimming or "cheese-paring" staff without terminating activities altogether — have thrown up a lot of savings. Although it is difficult to come by accurate figures, a report from the then Civil Service Department to the Treasury Select Committee in June 1981 showed that of a total manpower cut of 26,860 between 1st April 1980 and 1st April 1981, 12,188 (45 per cent) were due to "General streamlining (including lower standards of service) and other minor changes". In the same period, 1,517 jobs (6 per cent) went as a result of privatistion and another 601 due to hiving-off functions to new or existing public bodies.* These savings were achieved by a

---

* Treasury and Civil Service Committee "Civil Service Manpower Reductions", 12th July 1981, HOC 423.

Increasing militancy in the Civil Service; Blackpool, 1981 SCPS Conference demonstration.

combination of measures such as recruitment freezes, changes in staff inspection (complementing) procedures, and freezing individual posts.

However, it was increasingly the case that not only would 'cheese-paring' fail to achieve cuts on the scale demanded, but that the consequences of weakening services across the board by 'streamlining' methods could not go forever unnoticed. In their 1980 Report on Manpower Reductions, the influential Treasury and Civil Service Committee had already commented:

"We recognise that, while across the board cuts may well increase efficiency, this is likely to be only at the earlier stages of a major programme of manpower reductions such as now being carried out by the Government in reducing manpower by over 100,000. Across the board cuts are effective in removing any fat there may be but thereafter it is likely that significant reductions can only be achieved by abolition or reduction of services. We are concerned that the inability to express the 102,000 net contraction in the size of the Civil Service in terms of tasks to be either cut or reduced represents a weakness in the Government's policy. Unlike the December 1979 announcement, which detailed where the savings were to be made, the May 1980 announcement appears to have been a mainly political decision based on intention rather than on calculation."*

The Government's other great hope for achieving its manpower targets was the much-vaunted programme of scrutinies under the aegis of Sir Derek Rayner. But this was also failing to deliver the number of savings his admirers would have wished. The most complete review of Rayner's work was the White Paper on "Efficiency in the Civil Service" published in June 1981.** This paper was most notable for the paucity of real savings achieved. It also reported that "savings possibilities" of 11,000 had been identified, but that Ministers had been able to make firm decisions on only 3,000. The prospects of Rayner scrutinies alone coming up with the requisite number of "efficiency savings" were increasingly poor.

In an untypically facetious, but highly revealing review, the journal *Public Money* made the following comment on this paper:

"Costs to central government have been reduced by cutting the quality of service and increasing the risk of fraud. But that will just have to be accepted."***

The problem of reliance upon "cheese-paring" methods was most clearly put by Sir Geoffrey Otten, Second Permanent Secretary at the DHSS when he appeared before the Public Accounts Committee in July 1981. Commenting on the possibilities

* Treasury and Civil Service Committee "Civil Service Manpower Reductions", 22nd July 1980, HOC 712-1.
** "Efficiency in the Civil Service", Cmnd. 8293 July 1981.
*** *Public Money*, December 1981, pp.8-15.

for manipulating his department's complementary machinery he said:

"The annual score of savings that we can expect from staff inspection in DHSS is something in the region of 200 or 300. Staff Inspection is not a weapon for enabling us to find 16,000 staff savings by 1984. We are in a much bigger business where staff inspection is really rather a marginal tool. It is important for other reasons, but it does not get at these functions. The real thrust of all of our activities is towards cutting out a substantial block of work, which means legislation on, for instance, a new sick pay scheme, a new kind of housing benefit, possibly a simplified supplementary benefit scheme."*

His view was immediately supported by the Civil Service's own efficiency-policeman, the Comptroller and Auditor General, Sir Douglas Henley. He told the Committee:

"I do think it quite important for the Committee and anyone else who is interested, to be aware of the nature and limitations of staff inspection and various complementing controls in relation to these wider approaches to the need for a particular manpower level".**

The emerging picture was that the Civil Service was not in fact the dustbin of pen-pushers doing pointless tasks that some anti-public sector campaigners would have the public believe. The squeeze had been put on "waste and inefficiency" through cash limits initially, then through departmental manpower ceilings, distorted staff inspection activities,*** and through individual and

---

* Public Accounts Committee Sixth Report 1981/2, "Control of Civil Service Manpower", Par.3023.

** Public Accounts Committee Sixth report 1981/2, "Control of Civil Service Management", Par.3030.

*** A graphic example of how supposedly objective staff inspection procedures can be influenced by pressure to achieve cuts comes from the figures for inspections in the HQ and Development Divisions of the Overseas Development Administration:

Inspection Period	Posts Inspected (all grades)	Net Reduction in Posts	Per Cent of Inspected Post Cut
November 1976-October 1977	404½	0	0
November 1977-October 1978	355	½	0.1
November 1978-October 1979	277½	8½	3.1
November 1979-October 1980	602½	101	16.8

It would be difficult to argue that the demands of the "Soames Cuts" announced on 6th December 1979, did not play some part in the changed results of staff inspection in ODA. The great majority of the 1979/80 reductions were made in the messengerial and clerical grades in the office services area which clearly contradicted the Official Side's "explanation" that the dramatically changed figures reflected the reduction in bilateral aid programme activity.

service-wide scrutinies under Sir Derek Rayner. But, as Sir Geoffrey Otten spelled out to the Treasury Committee, services would have to go if the manpower targets were to be met. This is the third imperative for privatisation and hiving-off in the Civil Service. Staff in post numbers have to be pulled down somehow, even if, as later examples show, it is more expensive in the short- and long-term, to say nothing of changes in quality and effectiveness of the service delivered. For local authorities, cost remains the central determinant of decisions about privatisation, whatever problems and inadequacies there may be in the comparison of contract and direct costs. In central government, the priority is the 1984 manpower ceiling, and considerations about achieving the most economic use of public money are being sacrificed to this end. The rest of this paper sketches out current privatisation initiatives within the Civil Service and elaborates this point further.

Property Services Agency

The DoE, including the Property Services Agency (PSA) and the Department of Transport (DTp) makes a good starting point, both because of the range of activities to be privatised, and the enthusiasm with which the then Secretary of State for the Environment Michael Heseltine, has gone about shedding staff and services by all available means. On 1st April 1979, staff in DoE/PSA numbered 50,412. By 1st April 1982 this figure had fallen to 38,956, a reduction of 11,456 or 22 per cent — very nearly the total cut required by April 1984.* Of this reduction, about 5,250 (46 per cent) are accounted for by privatisation.**

PSA design work

The PSA was established in 1972 to provide property management services including building, construction, maintenance and supplies for the Government estate covering dockyards, airfields, prisons, courts, laboratories, computer centres and local offices. It is Britain's largest employer of construction industry skills.

Design work for major new installations had, until 1981, been shared between the PSA itself (two-thirds) and the private sector (one-third). In June 1981, the Secretary of State reversed this ratio,

* *Hansard,* 18th May 1982, Col.73.
** *Hansard,* 18th June 1982, Col.354.

giving two-thirds of design work to the private sector, in order to cut design staffing from 2,500 to 1,600. This decision was taken in spite of the fact that a working group (Semple/Sweet) including several big names from industry had already been commissioned to

March 1982, CPSA members from the PSA join a demonstration against the collapse of the building industry.

examine the in-house/out-house ratio. The final report of the Semple/Sweet Group will probably never be published, although it was widely suspected in the DoE that the Report would have favoured the existing arrangement with only one-third of design work going outside.

Apprentice training

A serious by-product of the decision to reverse the two-thirds/one-third ration has been a drastic cut in trainees within the PSA. An additional reason for the reduction is that trainees count as staff and cutting their numbers contributes towards targetted manpower reductions.

The PSA training scheme involves four years of study at local colleges and with the PSA's own tutors, leading to TEC Certificate and the TEC Higher Certificate. In 1979, the PSA planned to take on 530 trainees. Because of the recruitment freeze, only 165 were employed. For 16-year old school leavers, the Department had planned to offer 250 places in five courses leading to full qualification as technical assistants in architecture, civil engineering, quantity surveying, or as draughtsmen. Because of the freeze only 41 were taken on. In 1980 this figure rose to 65, but fell back in 1981 to 36, against a target set in 1979 of 390. In 1982 the PSA is offering just 135 training places, despite the Government's own emphasis on training, especially for recent school-leavers as set out in the *New Training Initiative* White Paper.

PSA Supplies

The PSA Supplies organisation exists to provide Government departments and other public authorities with a wide range of commodities including furniture, engineering equipment, building materials and heating fuel. It is a "trading fund" which means it has the worst of all worlds. Under the Government Trading Funds Act of 1973, the Supplies Division has to break even, by selling its goods at 'commericial' prices to client departments. However, it cannot operate as a private company would: it cannot pick and choose the commodities it wishes to trade in. It cannot delete "non-profitable" products or places of distribution. Purchasing is determined by Government policy; it cannot expand into new markets and cannot use any profit for future investment — any surplus goes back to the Treasury. Hence, at a time of major cut-backs in client departments and lack of money for investment, plus staff cuts, sales fell in many supplies areas, and previously profitable areas become loss makers.

In June 1981 the Environment Secretary approved five major cut-backs as follows:

- Central Engineering Workshop, Burtonwood — run-down of the rotating machinery section because of "dramatic decline in the amount of maintenance work available, particularly on heavy diesel generating plant"* as more maintenance contracts went to outside suppliers. One hundred industrial redundancies.

- Commercial Transport Fleet — closure following estimated £980,000 deficit in 1981/82. This deficit, from a near break-even in 1980/81 was due to HMSO being put under pressure to act on a trading fund basis, and reducing its payments to PSA for compact stationery loads, which had effectively cross-subsidised bulkier and less profitable loads of furniture etc. The decision to close was made despite a study commissioned by the Supplies Division from National Carriers Ltd., at a cost of £8,200, which would have returned the fleet to profitability even in the difficult circumstances in which it is forced to operate. The Division admitted that "strengthening the management team" and investment of £300,000 would be necessary, and that this would not be forthcoming. The entire operation went to private road hauliers with a loss of 140 drivers and porter jobs.

- Central Vehicle Workshops — The PSA formerly operated seven workshops around the country in order to maintain the supplies fleet and mobile plant. In the words of a management report on the workshops:

  "Since 1979, however, staff numbers have declined. The result has been a reduced through-put at each of the workshops and as overhead costs have remained fairly static, profitability has been adversely affected."**

The Environment Secretary felt that the work of the four less profitable workshops in Edinburgh, York, Burtonwood and Biggleswade, "...... could be carried out by private sector garages". The closure entailed 80 redundancies in industrial grades, although "the Secretary of State has said that he would

---

* Letter from PSA Supplies Division to Trade Union Side 26th June 1981.
** Background Paper to PSA Trade Union Side 3rd August 1981.

be prepared to consider offers to take over any of the workshops as a going concern either by a private firm or by a worker co-operative".*

● London Furniture Workshop — The workshops, employing 203 industrial grades including 138 porters and joiners, provide a portering and removals service for Government Departments in the Whitehall area. Again, in management's own words:

> "Over the last year, because of the reduced funds available to client departments, idle time has become an increasing problem in all activities except for porters and joiners who operate from client buildings . . . It was decided on efficiency and economy grounds to close the operation completely, and contract out all the services, except for a small force of about 20 people to provide an on the spot service in the Palace of Westminster and certain other nearby buildings."**

● Hayes Furniture Store — This store was used to assemble furnishings going overseas. Management asserted that "private freight forwarding firms who are expert in the business" could provide the service more cheaply, and closed the store with the loss of 30 industrial jobs.

In all, these five cuts in the Supplies Division contributed 540 jobs towards Heseltine's 1984 target. They were all justified on grounds of "economy". The other side of that coin is the downward spiral of performance, morale and profitability that is now common in much of the public sector. Forced to operate in an unreasonably restrictive environment, with no scope for investment or expansion, deficits increase, until what is in reality a highly desirable area of work can be laid in the lap of the private sector, described as a saving of public money and of course, a further reduction of civil servant numbers.

PSA Estates work

The major work of the PSA Estates Division is the allocation of accommodation to other Government Departments, including space planning, partitioning and service charge collection. PSA management consider that several areas of work in Estates could be privatised and have set up a series of "experiments" to test the

* Letter from PSA Supplies Division to Trade Union Side 26th June 1981.
** Background Paper to PSA Trade Union Side 3rd August 1981.

ability of the private sector to take on the work.

Consultants have been brought in on a trial basis to carry out space planning in offices in Croydon. The work of allocating service charges for Government premises is being considered for a similar experimental scheme. Outside London, private firms are being approached to carry out valuations for rent reviews on the Government estate. If these agencies are able to produce valuations close to those of the PSA's own staff, many hundreds of jobs will be endangered, as decisions could then be made to put valuation work out to contract. Rent reviews on agricultural land owned by the MoD are now partly carried out by private agencies. In London, the task of finding suitable new premises for unemployment benefit offices was put out to private agencies at the end of 1981, although their performance to date is understood to have been very poor. Cartographic services are now partly provided by agencies, although the attempt to privatise oil pipeline compensation work has foundered in the absence of firms equipped to work in such a specialised field.

To date, privatisation in the Estates Division has not disposed of many staff, although the potential loss, especially on rent review work may be substantial. Of more immediate concern is the use of outside agencies to cover for serious staff shortages. Cartographic services and the Estates London Region in particular, are well under complement following the various staff-cutting exercises. There have been no proper comparisons of the costs of using agencies as against the PSA's own staff. Decisions to put work outside are made in order that essential tasks can be carried out despite staff shortages arising from arbitrary manpower targets and with no concern at all about the increased costs that private contracts usually entail.

PSA Advisory Board

Not content with his own ability to achieve the privatisation of major aspects of PSA work, in December 1980 Secretary of State Michael Heseltine established the "PSA Advisory Board". The Board's terms of reference are "To review aspects of the PSA's procedures and policies as agreed from time to time with the Secretary of State and to report to him." The precise role of the Advisory Board was never clear, although *Building Magazine* seemed to have few doubts when it wrote, shortly after the Board came into existence: "The Chairman of the newly-appointed PSA Advisory Board will be telling the Environemtn Secretary that there is a need to reduce the size of thepublic sector and in particular current public spending, as opposed to capital expenditure".*

The composition of the Board might well have led *Building Magazine* to risk some other predictions about its likely intentions. The Board Chairman is Mr G.N. Mobbs of Slough Estates and the Charterhouse Group. Other members include Mr N.C. Baker of Taylor Woodrow; Mr B.J. Hill of Higgs and Hill Ltd. and Mr P. Radford of Stag Furniture Holdings. All these companies have made donations either to Conservative Party funds directly, or to British United Industrialists which has close links with the Tory Party.

Department of Transport

Heavy Goods Vehicle Testing

On 7th August 1980, the then Secretary of State for Transport (Mr Fowler) published proposals for the future of annual testing of heavy goods vehicles and public service vehicles. He said that he intended to transfer the network of 91 heavy goods vehicle testing centres to a limited number of private sector companies, who would also take on the annual testing of large passenger vehicles. "I believe that there is no case for retaining vehicle testing in the public sector, and employing a large number of civil servants, when the private sector can provide a more flexible and efficient service without any lowering of safety standards" he said. This proposal threatened 900 Civil Service jobs.

The Government proposed to group the existing network of testing stations into a number of chains which would be offered for sale to private sector companies. The companies would be free to use the centres to provide additional facilities for haulage operators alongside the testing facilities, such as maintenance and repair. They would also be allowed to apply for permission to set up new centres equipped to the prescribed standards. In grouping centres for disposal, the government aimed to introduce an element of competition between chains of centres. It was intended that vehicle operators would have a choice between centres under different

---

* *Building Magazine,* 20th February 1981.

ownership. The centres would also cater for testing of public service vehicles at operators' premises. The Government proposed to retain control over the content of the test and test procedures, but also said it was prepared to consider authorising tests from centres outside the chains.

The Government's proposals were considered by the Select Committee on Transport which reported in July 1981.* The various bodies in the road haulage industry all had major reservations about the proposals. The impartiality of the testing system would be put at risk, commercial malpractice would occur and standards of vehicle safety would fall, they felt. The Committee commented that vehicle operators were generally content with the service provided by the testing stations. They concluded that the government had not justified the contention that private operators would carry out the annual inspection system better than the existing Department of Transport testing stations. The Committee believed that, until the Department could bring forward evidence to substantiate their contentions, the existing system of HGV testing stations should be retained. The Committee concluded that if the Department of Transport insisted on privatisation of the system, the network should be taken over by either Lloyd's Register or some other organisation of "significant standing".

Despite the criticisms of the Transport Committee, the Government went ahead with enabling legislation in the 1982 Transport Bill. The Bill's provisions were wide, allowing the Secretary of State to implement whatever arrangement he is finally able to make with the private sector concerns. He has the power to authorise both companies as testing authorities and individuals within those companies.

On 24th May 1982, the Secretary of State told the House that agreement had been reached with Lloyd's Register on the establishment of a new association under its control, to undertake HGV and PSV testing. Three weeks later, however, it was clear that the Department was still having difficulty convincing anyone at all, including Lloyd's, that the idea was a good one. On 16th June the following exchange took place at Question time:

> "Mr Bagier: Will the Minister say what difference in impartiality will result from handing over this responsibility to Lloyd's Register? Since, during the Committee stage of the Bill, it was apparent to most of us in

---

* Fourth Report of the Transport Committee 1980-81 HOC 344.

Committee that Lloyd's Register was not interested in this, what carrots have been held out to cause it now to favour taking over?

"Mrs Chalker: Following the Committee debate, there has been a rethink, and Lloyd's Register has come forward with sensible suggestions for taking over the testing of heavy goods vehicles and public service vehicles. The industry is already being consulted through the Vehicle Operators' Advisory Panel, and Lloyd's Register has made this offer, which I am sure will bring improvements in flexibility and benefit for vehicle operators in the hours of testing. We hope to see a pilot project before long to make sure that the provisions which Lloyd's Register vehicle testing association expects to employ work thoroughly and well."*

The idiocy of the scheme, and opposition from all quarters has at present reduced wholesale privatisation plans for the 91 centres to "a pilot project before long to make sure that the provisions . . . work thoroughly and well."

Department of Environment

District Audit Service

The District Audit Service presently employs about 550 people to audit local authorities, water authorities and passenger transport executives in England and Wales. Proposals currently before Parliament in the Local Government Finance Bill recommend establishing an Audit Commission to be responsible for dividing up work between its own auditors and the private sector.

At present, local authorities have the freedom to use private sector auditors if they so wish, but the great majority choose to employ the District Audit Service. The main reason for this is that local authority accounting is a complex and specialised field, for which District Auditors are highly trained, qualified and experienced. Apart from the lack of comparable organisations in the private sector, the recent growth of value-for-money (VFM) auditing in the public sector, leaves private agencies even less equipped to take over this work.

Private sector auditors would inevitably bring a different attitude to their work than the Government service. In a nutshell, the private sector thinks mainly in terms of profit and loss, which are only part of the considerations of local authorities, which must be concerned with 'non-profitable' activities and concepts such as quality and effectiveness of service and equity in the treatment of

* *Hansard,* 16th June 1982, Col.944.

the public. Privatisation of audit work may compromise the impartiality that auditing of public finances demands.

An additional danger is that the proposed Audit Commission, in the grant of the Secretary of State, could be used to police politically difficult problems. Whilst the private sector may make substantial profit from routine work, the Commission staff could be ordered in to deal with "high spending" authorities for instance, compromising what is presently an independent service, where auditors are required to use their own professional judgment, free from political pressure.

Ancient Monuments and Historic Buildings

Within the Department of Environment, the Directorate of Ancient Monuments and Historic Buildings is responsible for the statutory protection of buildings and monuments, paying grants to owners, and maintaining the government's own properties. Over 2000 staff are presently employed in the Directorate, including craft workers, technicians, custodians and administrators.

The Environment Secretary has decided to hive-off the Directorate to a new agency to be launched in October 1983 or April 1984. Part of the agency's brief will be to make the DoE's monuments more commercially viable. This is certainly achievable. The larger tourist attractions can be made more profitable in a variety of ways: by charging policy, sale of franchises etc. The first question is whether it is right, or desirable, to attempt to maximise financial return from the nation's heritage. A more serious problem is that less famous or attractive landmarks will not have the same up-keep priority as the money-spinners. Other activities will also suffer. Outside organisations have criticised the decision to hive off monuments work because of this danger of reduced attention being paid to the heritage as a whole. The Council for British Archaeology, in evidence on the Secretary of State's consultative paper*, said "In view of the inadequate attention given to the organisation and role of scheduling of ancient monuments, listing of historic buildings, rescue archaeology and the Ancient Monuments Laboratory, the Council does not feel able to approve the proposals as presented". The changed priority of the agency is clear from the fact that the English Tourist Board

---

* "Organisation of Ancient Monuments and Historic Buildings in England" HMSO November 1981.

welcomed the new approach, calling for marketing staff to increase and improve the publicity given to those sites of interest to the tourist market.

Hiving off is a valuable way of cutting 2,000 Department staff. It means that the Administration will be financially vulnerable however and priority will shift from ensuring the up-keep of historic properties and sites as a whole, to concentrating on those where a return can be expected.

The Environment Secretary's personal commitment to privatisation had originally led him to consider the privatisation of the entire royal parks service, along with the Ancient Monuments Directorate. This idea was vetoed by the Lord Chamberlain and never officially saw the light of day!

Hydraulics Research Station

The Hydraulics Research Station employed 258 people working on a variety of projects including the Severn barrage, pollution, wave behaviour and flooding. It was considered to be one of the top three centres of civil engineering hydraulics in the world. In 1981, the Environment Secretary decided to convert the Station into a company limited by guarantee. Under a newly constituted Board, the Station is now independent of the Civil Service, but does not have private shareholders. The new company was given, without payment, the existing land and capital assets of the Station.

Countryside Commission

The Countryside Commission has been hived off from the DoE under the Wildlife and Countryside Act 1981. 101 staff were transferred to the new Commission.

Ministry of Defence

Royal Ordnance Factories

The Royal Ordnance Factories (ROFs) are responsible for manufacturing arms and munitions for the British armed forces and for sale abroad. They currently employ over 19,000 people in eleven establishments. Seven are engineering factories, two carry out ammunition filling and two manufacture explosives.

Since 1st July 1974, the ROFs have operated as a trading fund under the Government Trading Funds Act 1973 (like PSA Supplies). Performance has been consistently good. The Factories have succeeded in generating sufficient funds to maintain a healthy investment and expansion programme in addition to meeting financial targets set for them.

Despite their record, ROFs operate under commercial constraint, similar to those for PSA Supplies, as a result of the Trading Fund Status. The Government are now using these constraints as the justification for outright privatisation. On 20th May 1982 Defence Secretary John Nott announced in a Written Answer that "the ROFs should no longer operate under the Government Trading Funds Act 1973, but in a more commercial environment under the Companies Acts"* Initially the Government will continue to own

* *Hansard*, 20th May 1982, Col.151.

164

the factories but only as a transitional step towards privatisation.

In evidence to the Study Group set up to look at the ROFs in 1981, the Trade Unions put forward several ways in which the already sound trading position of the factories could be improved further. The Unions proposed that ROFs should have more responsibility for research and development work, that there should be more freedom in procurement and in pay and complementing. Further improvements in productivity and use of new technology were also offered, to be complemented by a new in-house sales and marketing unit to make the most effective use of output. Despite these not inconsiderable offers, the Government has preferred a two-stage process via a trading fund leading potentially to full private control over the British arms industry.

The immediate consequence of private ownership is that producers will concentrate on only the more profitable munitions and equipment. At present, the ROFs cannot refuse orders from the MoD. They are required to produce what the armed forces demand to the requisite design and standard, and in the right quantity at the right time. If full privatisation is achieved, operational necessity may become secondary to commercial viability.

Claims Commission

The MoD Claims Commission is responsible for dealing with civil claims against the MoD at home and abroad. It also deals with claims against visiting forces in the UK, and claims against most Civil Ministries arising from traffic accidents. The Commission has 180 staff. Expenditure on claims is about £10m per year.

Following a Rayner Scrutiny of the Commission in 1980, a three-year contract for third-party traffic accident work and employer's liability was let to General Accident to run from 1st April 1982. Over three years 80 jobs will be lost in the Commission as a result.

In deciding to privatise, the Government argued that financial savings were the prime motive.However, publication of figures comparing contract price with in-house cost have been refused. The MoD trade unions have argued that this refusal stems either from the fact that the proposal will prove to be expensive, or that the General Accident tender could be shown to be a "loss leader". After three years, when staff and skills in the Claims Commission have been run down, and with no other private firms with the necessary experience, General Accident will be in a strong position to re-negotiate a further contract on terms more attractive to itself.

Aside from the dubious financial considerations there are few safeguards for claimants in the privatisation proposal. In particular, MP's representations and Parliamentary Questions on claims cases will cease to be an immediate avenue for claimants who are unhappy with standards of service.

Quedgeley Accommodation Stores

The MoD Accommodation Stores at Quedgeley near Gloucester are responsible for providing non-military equipment and supplies for all three services. The Defence Secretary has decided that this work should be handed over to private contractors with a loss of 495 industrial and non-industrial jobs.

Museums

It is understood that MoD Museums may be included in the forthcoming Museums Bill, changing their status to trustee-controlled institutions.

The Museums affected are:
- National Army Museum   66 posts
- RAF Museum   90 posts

(The Battle of Britain Museum and RAF Aerospace Museum at Cosford are subsidiaries of the RAF Museum, and have directly employed staff, but it is understood that these museums will not be included in the Bill.)

- Portsmouth Royal Naval Museum   23 posts
- Royal Marines Museum   26 posts

The Fleet Air Arm Museum and the Submarine Museum are also under consideration for inclusion in the Bill, but in the main the staff are not civil servants, so their inclusion would add nothing to the cull. Nor is it likely that the Regimental and Corps Museums will be included.

There will be changes in the way the museums are funded, and they would be able to charge for admission in order to raise extra funds. It is expected that the museums will be funded by grant-in-aid and that the MoD will continue to provide most of the present supporting services. At present there is no intention to change the legal status of the museums, since under the Charities Act and their charters they may already act on their own behalf and employ staff.

The position on staff is not clear. Since most are specialists it is unlikely that they will be re-absorbed elsewhere in the MoD and will, therefore, be offered jobs with the museums. Decisions have still to be taken whether the offers of employment will be on comparable terms and whether, like the trustee museums, these museums will be scheduled under the Superannuation Act 1972, so that staff remain members of the Civil Service Pension Scheme.

Other MoD Functions

Proposals are rapidly developing in a number of other MoD areas including:

- Royal Aircraft Establishment (RAE) West Freugh — privatisation of 12 + posts at test range from mid-July 1982.

- RAE Llanbedr — 4 + posts lost to private contractor.

- RAE Farnborough — possible effect on jobs through opening up field to civilian flying.

- RAE Wind Tunnels — feasibility study in train on contracting out wind tunnel work.

- National Gas Turbine Establishment — feasibility study in train on handing some or all of NGTE Pyestock work over to Rolls Royce, who are already involved.

- Military Vehicles Engineering Establishments, Christchurch and Kircudbright — feasibility study in train on contracting out bridge-testing and test-range work. 62 + posts at risk.

Contract Cleaning

The Government has repeatedly argued that contract cleaning is more economical than using directly employed cleaning staff. Although there is now substantial evidence to the contrary, the basis for comparison has been a major source of dispute and the unwillingness of Government departments to assess the full cost of privatisation continues to make analysis of relative cost difficult in many cases.

It is a stated requirement that contract firms should pay the local authority rate as a minimum. There is evidence that this condition is not always met. Private firms are also free of any obligation to provide pension or shift allowance benefits to their staff. Substantial increases in workload are also common in the private sector: whilst the recommended work-rate for a Civil Service cleaner is 1350-1450 square feet per hour, contractors have been bidding for Government contracts at figures of 2,400 square feet an hour. The job of "cleaning" includes stairs and toilets, emptying ashtrays and waste-bins, dusting and polishing furniture ledges, pipes and skirtings as well as vacuuming, sweeping or polishing floors. The inclusion of increased work rates in tenders means either that contractors will provide a poorer service or they will take advantage of the fact that cleaning staff are predominantly part-time women difficult for trade unions to organise, and easy to exploit.

The major hidden cost to the Exchequer of contract cleaning is the lost income from insurance contributions. If cleaning employers can manipulate their employees' hours so that earnings remain below the national insurance threshold, the firm avoids liability for employers' contributions. The Civil Service Union has evidence that over and above restricting the number of hours worked, some firms employ the "sleeper" technique — paying salary cheques in non-existent names — in order to evade NI payment. The CSU estimates that if all Government work were handed over to private contractors, the loss of revenue would be in the order of £1m per annum.

Another factor is the cost to departmental cash-limited budgets of paying 15 per cent VAT on cleaning contracts. Whilst this money theoretically returns to the Exchequer and there is no net spending, the fact is that VAT has to be accounted for within the departmental cash limit and savings have to be found elsewhere.

These factors escape consideration when cost comparisons are made. Despite this loading of the balance sheet in favour of private firms, the recent decision by the Manpower Services Commission not to use direct cleaning for its new headquarters at Moorfoot in Sheffield is a vivid example of the ability of direct cleaning to compete financially and of the importance of manpower targets in the decision-making process.

The Civil Service Unions had proposed that the MSC building be cleaned by direct labour. Costings were submitted showing that this could be done economically. The CSU also proposed to adjust its proposals, if necessary, to come below any private tender. The following quote comes from the MSC's 'final' reply to the CSU's bid:

"We have given you as much information about the accepted tender as we are permitted to give and I hope you will accept that in monetary terms there was very little to choose between you and the chosen firm.

"It would however be misleading of me to imply that we had taken little account of the manpower repercussions. To have accepted the CSU bid would have entailed the employment of an additional 84 part-time staff which under the current 'rules' would have counted as 42 full-time staff. We are by no means clear precisely how Corporate Services Division will attain its reduced staff objective for the last year of the cuts (83/84) and we could not therefore have contemplated taking on another 42 staff since this could only have led directly to the withdrawal of equal numbers of front-line staff providing services to the public. We could not even contemplate putting such a proposal to Commissioners. Had we had direct cleaning in London, no such problem would have arisen; the posts could have been 'transferred'.

"In summary, there was really very little financially between your bid and that of the firm we have accepted — a matter of pounds in a contract worth some £80,000 per annum.

"I regret have to write in these terms but I do not see that I had any choice given the constraints within which we are working."*

The message is clear: the CSU's proposal might be cheaper despite the private sector's "hidden cost" advantages, but the 1984 manpower target is paramount and economy can be sacrificed accordingly.

The major loss of cleaning jobs through privatisation has been in the *Ministry of Defence* where firm decisions to bring in contractors have been taken, or already implemented, for 4,700 out of approximately 7,000 cleaners. The great majority of these cleaners are in industrial grades. The MoD has a rolling programme of feasibility studies in train, the eventual result of which will be the virtual abolition of direct cleaning in the department.

In the *Inland Revenue,* 365 non-industrial cleaning jobs have gone in 85 out of 162 offices examined. Other areas where cleaning is threatened with privatisation include: Metropolitan Police, Scottish Office, DHSS, Dept. of Employment and Customs & Excise.

Department of Health and Social Security

Employers' Statutory Sick Pay

Although "privatisation" has generally referred to the transfer of a discrete function, including capital assets, to either one or a small number of private companies, the decision to shuffle off on to

* Letter from MSC Corporate Services division to CSU, 12th June 1981.

employers the responsibility for payments for the first eight weeks of sickness, may also be seen as a privatisation.

The Housing and Social Security Benefits Bill containing the Employers Statutory Sick Pay (ESSP) proposals received Royal Assent on 28th June 1982, and the ESSP provisions will be in force from April 1983. In essence, employers, rather than the DHSS, will be responsible for making sick payments to employees for the first eight weeks they are sick in any one tax year. This covers the majority of sick absences. The Act lays down three rates of ESSP entitlement according to earnings, and a mechanism whereby employers can deduct monies paid from their National Insurance Contributions.

The prime motive behind ESSP is staff cuts, as Sir Geoffrey Otten told the Public Accounts Committee.* The Government was prepared to force the legislation through despite determined opposition from their own supporters in the small business community who opposed the scheme because of both the administrative burden it will place upon them and the financial consequences of having to pay employers' contributions on ESSP payments for which they will not be compensated. The Government went so far as to overturn a Committee stage amendment removing the requirement for employers' contributions because of the loss of income it entailed. Despite the refusal to make this concession, the savings to the Government from the scheme as a whole are neglible, and potentially negative. In the Financial Memorandum attached to the Bill** an overall loss of approximately £170m was predicted, although the decision to treat sickness (and unemployment) benefit as earnings, and hence liable for tax and national insurance, is expected to provide about £200m from ESSP payments — a small net profit to the Exchequer.

The manpower cut in DHSS as a result of removing the major responsibility for sickness benefit will be about 5,000 staff, mostly low paid clerical officer and clerical assistant grades. About 1,500 officers will be required, however, to carry out checks on employers' operation of the scheme, and in particular on deductions from national insurance payments. This work entails higher grade staff being retrained or recruited, at some extra cost,

---

* Public Accounts Committee Sixth Report 1981/2, "Control of Civil Service Manpower", Par.3023.
** "Housing and Social Security Benefits Bill" Financial Memorandum November 1981.

although moves are currently afoot in the Department to downgrade N.I. inspection work to clerical officer level, in an attempt to reduce costs. The major hidden loss, however, will be instances of accidental and deliberate over-retention of NI payments which the Government itself has admitted are the main dangers of the 100 per cent deduction scheme adopted. In their June 1981 consultative paper on compensation for employers, the DHSS said:

> "There have been suggestions that compensation should take the form of 100 per cent self-deductions . . . Even if the number of visits to employers by DHSS inspectors were increased substantially . . . it is probable that monies would be withheld from the National Insurance Fund either erroneously, fraudulently or in respect of malingering; the inevitable consequences would be an increase in the employers' contribution rate. In effect, a 100 per cent self-deduction scheme could end up with the honest, efficient employer subsidising the dishonest, inefficient one. For those reasons the Government remain strongly opposed to this approach."*

Following pressure from large employers' organisations, notably the CBI, this was the scheme eventually chosen and the consequences may well be a net financial loss, despite benefit taxation, although the principal staff cut objective, at around 3,500, will have been achieved.

Ministry of Agriculture, Fisheries and Food

Cattle Breeding Centre, Shenfield — 30 posts

The proposal is to hand over the centre to a commercial artificial insemination organisation and to seek tenders for the transfer. A final decision will be taken by 1st October 1982 with a view to a formal hand over on 31st March 1983. It is not thought that any legislation is required. MAFF seems to be accepting that there will be some redundancy of civil servants.

Tubecular Production for Mamalian and TB Testing — 15 Posts

The proposal if to transfer the function to a commercial pharmaceutical company with the product being inspected by MAFF inspectors. No legislation is thought to be necessary and no date for the transfer has yet been set. It is thought the people currently involved will be redeployed elsewhere in MAFF.

---

* "Compensating Employers for Statutory Sick Pay — A Consultative Document" DHSS June 1981.

National Collections, Torry — 17 Posts

It is proposed to set up a new company which will be a subsidiary of a holding company — Aberdeen University Research and Industrial Services — of which Aberdeen Universities are the shareholders. The target date is the end of August or the beginning of September 1982.

Royal Botannic Gardens, Kew — 527 Posts

It is understood that Kew Gardens will also be included in the Museums Bill. It is intended that the gardens should be transferred to trustees and the target date is 1st April 1984.

Central Office of Information
Film Unit — 26 Posts

The COI Film Unit is being privatised in line with government policy and some 26 directors, production assistants and technicians have already been made redundant. Guarantees of work with other subcontractors have been given to technicians who have not obtained alternative employment.

Department of Education and Science
Science Museum and Victoria and Albert Museum

A Rayner scrutiny has recommended that both museums should become non-departmental and the Minister for the Arts has now decided that the museums will be given trustee status, similar to the British Museum. It is expected that the operative date for the change will be April 1984 though this has not yet been announced. Discussions have not yet started on terms and conditions although the staff will probably keep the same conditions of service as civil servants.

Department of Energy
Gas Meter Examiners — 10 Posts

Responsibility for meter inspections was passed to the manufacturers in April 1982. A total of 10 gas meter examiners were involved. All staff involved left the service and none were redeployed by the manufacturers.

Home Office

Residential Training Establishments

The contracting-out concerns the catering and housekeeping services at the Home Office's residential training establishments. The number of non-industrials involved is small — only two or three people per establishment — with the majority of the impact falling on industrial staff. So far the services at three colleges have been privatised. Two of the staff have been employed by the new contractors and all those affected have received appropriate redundancy compensation. Efforts are being made to redeploy the other four within the civil service, but it seems likely that they will have to be made redundant. The Home Office is now conducting privatisation studies at five further establishments.

Department of Industry

Computer Aided Design Centre — 6 Posts

The Centre only directly employs six civil servants, the rest of the employees being on contract from Data Skills (ICL). Although the number of civil service staff involved is small, the privatisation of CADC would mean a loss of capacity in the Computer Aided Design/Computer Aided Manufacture area where both NEDC and Advisory Council for Applied Research and Development have stated that a strategic government role is required. A privatised CADC would also have implications for other laboratories in DTI, particularly NEL, which at present collaborates closely with CADC. The decision on hiving-off has been made in principle but feasibility studies are still being produced.

National Maritime Institute — 270 Posts

The National Maritime Institute was formed in 1976 from the Ship and Maritime Science Divisions of the National Physical Laboratory. Present staff numbers are 270 and the Institute has three sites, at Feltham (Middlesex), Teddington (on the NPL site) and Hythe (Hampshire) on Southampton Water. The Institute carries out research, development and testing for both government and commercial organisations. The Institute also acts in an advisory role to government and is further funded for research work to maintain its capability.

The Government has decided to privatise the NMI from October

1982, under a shadow board, which, like the Hydraulics Research Station, will receive the NMI assets free or at a "peppercorn" rent. A substantial subsidy will still be required since the NMI cannot possibly be viable on its own account.

Royal Hospital, Chelsea — 200 Posts

This establishment became a grant-aided body on 1st April 1982.

Department of Agriculture and Fisheries for Scotland

Royal Botanic Gardens, Edinburgh

Legislation will be required to effect the transfer, although final decisions have apparently not yet been taken on the status of the new organisation. A feasibilty study was carried out 12 months ago which has never been released to the trade union side.

Royal Scottish Museum

The trade union side received a letter of 20th July 1982 telling them that the RSM will be given trustee status in line with the English Museums. In this case it is expected the hiving off will be effective from November 1984.

Civil Service pay

Whilst not falling strictly within the definition of privatisation two recent developments on the pay front are worthy of note.

Megaw Inquiry

Until its abolition in 1981, an independent body, the Pay Research Unit, had been responsible for preparing the job and pay data which formed the basis for pay negotiations in the Civil Service. The PRU was a body composed of civil servants seconded from a variety of Government departments. In 1978, the Pay Research Unit Board was established to oversee and ensure the independence of the PRU itself.

Following the abolition of the long-accepted Civil Service pay research process and the consequent 21 week Civil Service strike during 1981, the Government set up a Commission of Inquiry under the Chairmanship of Sir John Megaw to investigate methods of determining pay in the Civil Service. On 7th July 1982, the Megaw Committee published its findings. Whilst preserving a role for comparability in the pay determination process, the Committee proposed new data collecton methods under the auspices of a "Pay Information Board". Megaw proposes that data should be prepared, under the Board's instructions by management consultants:

> "We propose that, to maintain demonstrable independence from the Civil Service management and the unions, surveys, data collection and analyses should be undertaken by management consultants on behalf of the Board. Management consultants of suitable calibre will have the necessary experience of how private sector companies determine pay, and the availability of their data banks should reduce the amount of work which would need to be undertaken by a completely separate unit. They also have tried and tested systems of job evaluation and comparison which could probably be adapted for use in the Civil Service. They would be seen to be impartial."*

The Civil Service Unions have consistently opposed the use of management consultants. Whilst they may be "impartial" on some matters, pay for public servants certainly isn't one of them!

Private health care

The Government's pay offer to the non-industrial Civil Service in February 1982 generated a storm of protest over both the meanness and the discriminatory nature of the offer, ranging from 5½ per cent for people on scale maxima to zero per cent for staff on scale minima or age points.

Union anger over the pay component was matched, however, by its reaction to another proposal, under the heading "Other Improvements": — "The Government would be prepared to negotiate a group discount scheme for staff wishing to undertake private medical insurance at their own expense". Treasury officials said that civil servants agreeing to join the scheme "would benefit from 'advantageous discounts' negotiated between the Government and private medical firms such as BUPA".**

The offer was rejected out of hand by the Unions and the health insurance proposal has yet to re-emerge, although senior officials are known to be continuing discussions with medical insurance companies.***

---

* "Compensating Employers for Statutory Sick Pay — A Consultative Document" DHSS June 1981.

** "Inquiry into Civil Service Pay" Cmnd.8950, July 1982.

*** *Guardian,* 23rd June 1982.

Union responses

To date there has been little co-ordinated union action: where privatisation proposals have been successfully put off, there was additional pressure from industry or other consumer organisations against the proposal. Some services have become less attractive to the private sector because of cost-saving changes e.g. the introduction of voluntary registration at job centres means that the PER is now a less attractive proposition for private agencies. The Council of Civil Service Unions (CCSU) is currently discussing the responses to the growing threat of privatisation, including closer links with the industrial unions.

In the Department of Employment, the SCPS has involved members in developing an alternative to the MSC's corporate plan. Inevitably, much of the emphasis of the alternative plan has been upon defending existing services. It was suggested that for this sort of initiative a framework for new ideas has to be created, probably in small-scale education situations, although because of their position in union hierarchies, trade union researchers find it difficult to become involved in working with stewards at a local level.

Conclusion

Government initiatives to cut spending and manpower have increased in number and sophistication since May 1979. Against a back-drop of strict cash limits, the early recruitment freeze and across-the-board cuts were consolidated in fixed departmental staff-in-post targets for April 1984.

Some Civil Service functions, such as PSA Supplies, are suffering from reduced demand, because of cuts in public expenditure, and so become uneconomic and candidates for being hived off. The function of job centres is seen by Government as providing employers with work seekers. Currently there is less demand for workers, so job centres can be closed in some areas.

These examples can be considered in the light of increased emphasis on the importance of "reading across" the findings of individual Rayner scrutinies to other areas which has led to studies designed on a cross-departmental basis (Statistics, Use of Administrative Forms, Support Services for Research and Development Establishments). "Cost-conscious" drives together with the difficulty of meeting spending targets have accumulated in a major initiative to devolve responsibility for identifying and achieving cuts to lower tiers of management. Departments are under pressure to re-organise and develop local management accounting practices, whatever consequences this may have for quality and evenness of service across the country. National personnel agreements are under threat, as part of the aim of giving maximum budget flexibility to middle management. An important part of Rayner philosophy was detailed attention to spending at every level in a department, and despite the fading star of the one-function Rayner scrutiny as originally conceived, this element of his approach underpins current thinking on "local cost centres" and delegated management responsibility for spending and cuts. Management consultants, brought in by several departments to address the problem of extracting further savings from already-wasted services, came up with similar solutions (e.g. Cooper Lybrand in MAFF and Price Waterhouse in DHSS). Apart from his top-of-the-table position in respect of manpower cuts, Environment Secretary Heseltine has also been feted for his management information system, MINIS, which although of limited application outside his own Department, has inspired Ministers in their research for a management structure for "Whitehall Ltd".

These initiatives are aimed both at cutting staff and spending, and also at putting the implementation of Government policy on a strict business management footing, cleansed of awkward considerations such as quality of service or equity and fairness in the application of legislation. "Rough justice" is now quite acceptable in the application of law and policy, provided that spending is kept down.

The Government's achievements both in cash "savings" and in shift of ideology about the responsibilities of Administration are considerable. However the major problem remains that with trimming and "efficiency" savings exhausted, further major cuts are not easy to find. The political price of complete abolition of activities is often too high for the relatively small saving cutting any one function will enable. Privatisation is the ideal half-way house. Objectives for Government spending, numbers of civil servants and PSBR can be met whilst maintaining the activity in some form, and providing lucrative contracts for the Government's natural supporters in industry. To date, privatisation has accounted for a third of the 1984 manpower cut. In future it will be the principle method of continuing to cut the Civil Service.

9. Strategies to Fight Privatisation

Dexter Whitfield
(Services to Community Action and Tenants (SCAT))
Dave Hall,
(TURU Research Associate)

Introduction

One of the central aims of Tory strategy is a fundamental restructuring of the public services. This involves a massive transfer of assets and work to big business and the creation of a two-tier system of private and public provision. Just as we now have a two-tier system in housing, so the Tories want a similar system for health, education and social services.

Despite gaining more jobs, better working conditions and more public services over the last 35 years, the labour movement has not gained any real *control* over the running and quality of, nor investment in, public services. The last Labour government cut public spending — mainly on capital projects like council house building, schools, hospitals — hitting those using these services and the firms who gain from construction and equipment contracts. Now the Tories are seeking to drive down the number of jobs, wages and working conditions in the public services as well as restructuring them. It is not just the traditional 'welfare state' which is under attack but all public services run by local authorities, the NHS, nationalised industries, public bodies and central government. Further de-regulation including the scrapping of National Agreements (already happening in school meals), Wages Councils and possibly extending free enterprise zones throughout the economy are all part of the Tories' vision of more profitable and competitive industries and services.

While the Tories have a relatively clear vision of what they want to see, the labour movement increasingly pins its hopes on the Alternative Economic Strategy which pitifully lacks any vision about the public services. The AES hardly goes beyond demands for more public spending (falling precisely into the Tory trap of concentrating on money and what 'we can afford') or demands for re-nationalisation and more public ownership (the Tories are even capturing the use of terms like 'public ownership' — they mean private share ownership by a few members of the public as part of their ideological attack and a justification for the privatisation of state assets).

We think that the Tories intend to intensify their attack on the public services. We argue that the Tories' overtly political attack has to be met on the public front by an offensive from the labour movement. This means developing strategies which fight *for* improved and expanded public services and mounting an ideological counter-offensive arguing for the principles of public service. There are signs that new strategies, new organisations and new links between workers and users are taking root. Finally, we argue that although these initiatives are developing within the state, it is essential that workers and users develop plans, campaigns and organisations independently from the state.

Re-structuring the public services — the Tory attack

The Tories came into power in 1979 committed to selling off some of the state's assets and to 'roll back the frontiers of the public sector'. They set about re-organising and restricting services, introducing new legislation (10 new Acts/Bills give powers to privatise), changing controls, and creating the conditions to speed up privatisation. There are now five different forms of privatisation — the transfer of work and hiring of contractors to run services, the sale of publicly owned land and property, the sale of state owned companies and shares, allowing firms to exploit public services, and the introduction of private capital into public services.

Privatisation has played a central role in the Tories' economic and political strategy because it results in cuts in wages, benefits and working conditions by forcing workers to be employed by contractors instead of public bodies; it reduces the strength of the trade union movement becuase many private firms are not unionised; it lowers standards and expectations of public services forcing people to turn to private provision; it encourages conflict and reinforces divisions within the working class e.g. between public service workers and users; and it creates new markets for private industry. Cuts and changes in the pattern of public spending coupled with more centralised control have played a key part in this strategy.

The Tories are quickly moving from a position which, at least publicly, focussed on the mechanisms for privatisation and creating the right political climate to one where they are actively helping to create the alternative private provision. Their attempt to restructure the public services is now more explicit about creating a two-tier system of private and public provision in health, social services, education and other services.

The policies for the public sector don't stop at a shake out of jobs, wage cuts, and getting rid of 'waste' and 'inefficiency', but are also attempting to fundamentally change the nature of the services and who provides them. The Tories don't intend to dismantle services — a third rate public health service, third rate social services and a third rate education for working class people will perform the same residual and ideological function as council housing increasingly does for those who 'fail' and keep the rest competing to keep out of it. Nor are the Tories simply giving contracts, selling assets at knock-down prices or giving increased opportunities for speculation to their friends in business. Privatisation and the restructuring of public services is a clear strategy to concentrate more wealth in the hands of the wealthy. It covers all services — from the cradle to the grave — including those we all use regularly as well as those traditionally seen as part of the 'welfare state.'

Tory strategy has been articulated by Leon Brittain, Chief Secretary to the Treasury, who, speaking to the Institute of Fiscal Studies in May 1982, called for more involvement of the private sector in health, education and social services. He called into question the provision of free services like education and hinted at a two-tier system in which the government would finance a very basic provision of services and people would have to pay out of their pockets for anything above the basic service. "The fact that the financial provision may be made by the state does not mean necessarily that the goods have to be delivered in the public sector" stated Brittain. He has previously stated that he thought the government should model its public services on those in America.

This was followed in July 1982 by a speech by Sir Geoffrey Howe arguing that the core of the next Conservative election manifesto should focus on a large shift of public services to the private sector. He advocated further de-regulation of government controls, reform of the labour market coupled with privatisation in industry and public servces. Examples he gave included some private ownership of public utilities, transfer of local government functions to private firms, increasing use of charges, volunteers and firms in social services, the rapid expansion of private health facilities and insurance, 'community' financing of local schools and a voucher system to stimulate further expansion of private education — all presented under the guide of 'increased choice', 'greater freedom', 'healthy competition' etc.

This goes some way towards meeting the demands of a number of right-wing pressure groups, employers' organisations and companies who are waging a concerted and aggressive campaign to implement wide scale privatisation quickly.

Of course the government's strategy is not confined to privatising *existing* services but also ensuring that any *new opportunities* arising from new technology, e.g. the 'rewiring of Britain' and all the potential growth in communications, and the redevelopment of cities, e.g. London's Docklands, will be ruthlessly exploited by the private sector.

The parallel with housing noted above has other serious implications. There may be some services which the Tories may find it difficult, in political or practical terms, to privatise directly to contractors. In addition there may well be scandals as contracting out escalates and firms fail to provide the required services or refuse to renew contracts because the work is not profitable enough. In this situation the Tories may well develop the idea of an intermediary "third force", effectively outside the public sector, just as they did in the housing sector with housing associations (enthusiastically adopted by the Labour Government in 1974). The same arguments were used then as now about the "inefficiency", bureaucracy and unresponsiveness of services. A similar type of organisation to housing associations might be set up to take over parts of services, then government policy and funding would be constructed in such a way so as to channel funding and work to such organisations at the expense of public services. These organisations would, after a few years, be declared "successful'— exactly what has happened to housing associations. Such schemes would undoubtedly be strongly supported by the SDP and Liberals.

The other danger is the development of "third force" type ideas *within* the labour movement which would have many of the same effects as privatisation e.g. setting up co-operatives to take over services (some Liverpool Council refuse workers have already tried to develop such a scheme). Other schemes encouraging workers' and users' 'participation' with increased responsibllities and volunteerism may also find some support amongst certain sections because they may see this as the only way of retaining their jobs.

Prospects for public services in the 1980s

Whenever the general election is held it seems that if the Tories manage to maintain the present political climate they will probably win. Their ideological onslaught which has included attacking the concept and principles of public provision and service has contributed significantly to creating the conditions whereby not only could they win the next election but also gain a mandate for far-reaching changes in public services with a privatisation manifesto. What has happened so far is bad enough, but after another five years in which private enterprise is allowed to rip open public services like vultures gnawing at flesh, by 1990, the labour movement will hardly recognise the bones, never mind the body. All that will remain after a century of struggle will be the unprofitable scraps. The question is not how far they might succeed or want to go in this direction, but the fact is that this is the course they have set. Clearly, Tory strategy for the public services has grave implications for the labour movement.

How do we respond to this attack?

The response to cuts in public spending by the Labour Government was essentially defensive. Cuts campaigns, often combining public service unions, tenants and community groups, womens' organisations etc, took various forms of action under "stop the cuts" and "prevent the closure" slogans. This often involved occupations and other forms of direct action. The lessons from this period include:

- defensive demands alone are inadequate — they are usually limited to restoring things which were already inadequate.
- many people will not take part in action to defend services, although they might agree in principle with them, their regular experience is one of alienation, excessive red tape and long delays. They might be public services but they are not *their* services.
- unity between public service workers and users in essential.

● developing visions and alternatives beyond mere slogans about what public services should be like must play a crucial role in any action. The lack of such debate and discussion on any significant scale in the labour movement was exposed.

● reliance on traditional forms of industrial action in the public services is inadequate.

But the Tories have intensified and shifted the attack. It is not just cuts but also the *basic principles* of public services which are at stake. A defensive response which was inadequate between 1975-80 is even more inadequate now under the Tories' political and ideological attack.

We desperately need to adopt strategies which try to move the labour movement struggle on to the offensive. The difficulties can't be overstated particularly in a period when many workers lack confidence to take action, management are on the offensive and many workers are afraid of losing their jobs. However action in support of the health workers has shown that support can be gained for "just" causes. Any strategy must also recognise the problems in the public services — there is a lot wrong with many services and there always will be in public services run in a capitalist economy. We have to develop a better understanding of the contradictions, the positive and negative aspects of public services. The limitations can't be hidden. Anyway the Tories are currently using these problems, e.g. longer waiting lists, inadequate service, under-staffing etc. as reasons to hive them off to the private sector as opposed to improving and expanding services to help to iron out these problems.

Given this situation do we have any option other than to develop alternative offensive strategies? And what should these be like? Does our salvation lie in some form of the Alternative Economic Strategy (AES) combined with local economic and employment initiatives by left Labour local authorities?

Some important points about strategies

● *We have to try to move the terrain of the struggle away from the current focus on the cost of public services and the amount of public spending.* The scale, quality and *effectiveness* of services are what matters. Failure to do so will mean fighting the Tories on their own ground. We *can't* win on the costs argument in isolation. To do so will mean throwing out all national agreements on wages and conditions and taking massive job and wage cuts. The very nature of privatisation, particularly when there are four million unemployed, means that the private sector will invariably undercut the public sector when it resorts to bidding on contracts? We also have to challenge the crazy way that public spending and borrowing is valued, measured, organised and allocated, and to obliterate notions that it is "unproductive" and "parasitic".

We need to counter the Tories' ideological attack with education and propaganda arguing *for* the concept and principles of public services. This must involve building on the existing public support for the NHS and social services, recognising that there are problems but that these can be solved within the public sector, demanding radical improvements and new services, and drawing in support for other services in the process. This must be addressed equally to workers and to users. It requires a rapid shift by the trade union movement away from traditional economism and towards arguing as strongly and extensively for good quality services as for jobs, pay and conditions. It means countering the Tories' attempts to achieve a "reformed and de-politicised trade union structure" with a clear political response around which to organise.

● *We have to move beyond the simplistic demands for more public spending on health, housing, education etc.* All the variations of the AES and the TUC's alternative strategy call for increased public spending. Who bids £4bn? . . . £6bn over here! and so it goes on. Increased public spending is seen much more for what it can do for the economy (by boosting employment) and British industry than for the public services themselves. Clearly spending more in the same old way irrespective of whether it is on housing, health or social services will achieve little more than extra jobs, and given the proposed focus on capital spending, more contracts for industry. No doubt some of it will be spent training Cuts Restorers. And what qualitative differences will there be as a result of further nationalisation and the re-nationalisation of assets already sold off?

We urgently have to generate more rank and file debate and discussion about what kind of housing, health and other services tenants, workers and users want. We have to go beyond global figures of so many million pounds here or there and get down to people's needs and demands. Many workers and users already have ideas and visions about services and what they should be like, but need a framework and stimulus to develop them. Let's start, for a change, with the kind of services we want, their quality and availability, a good standard of pay and conditions for workers, how we should *control* the service, and then work out what they will cost and how they can be financed utilising all the available resources. This is not to argue the case for rank and filism at the expense of the development of ideas and policies at a wider lever. The two have to go hand in hand. The present situation sees the presence of "national" policies like the AES over which there are many fundamental questions, and the absence of anything else.

● *We need to develop new tactics to add a new dimension to traditional forms of industrial and community action in the public services.* We have to make issues about the scale, quality and availability of services much more up front, part of negotiating demands, and linked to pay and conditions. Industrial action in the public services while often having an economic impact on industry and the state as employer also has an equally important impact on the users of the service. The crunch is realising, harnessing and using that political dimension. Success may well depend on developing and strengthening joint action with users of services and the extent to which industrial and community action is made overtly political. That will mean confronting head-on the Tories' employment legislation. It also means not relying solely on traditional responses, e.g. always resorting to strike action, marches etc. For example, instead of the usual activists' march, time and resources could be used to get out to talk to people and distribute information and propaganda on estates and at workplaces. This often has less immediate and identifiable results but is crucial in the longer term for building the necessary political support. The Tories are waging a political offensive — we have to confront it head on.

● *We need to develop greater unity and more permanent working relationships and organisational links between public service workers and the users of services.* This is not "just a good thing" but an essential strategy. In addition the intensification of the Tories' attack on the pubic services will lead to further divisions and conflicts between workers, unemployed, and users pushing more women into the home with increased responsibilities for the health, education and caring of children, the elderly and those who are ill.

The last five years have seen links develop in some areas between civil servants and claimants, tenants and building workers, but this needs to be greatly expanded and strengthened both informally, through better links and coalitions between labour movement organisations, and through the setting-up of workers' and users' committees. The labour movement badly needs its own showpieces (just like the privatisation of the Southend refuse service has been exploited by the Tories and contractors) to act as a stimulus and example on our own terms.

Of course there are often conflicts of interests between workers and users in some services and these will not easily be resolved or minimised. To develop working relationships with users, setting up workers' and users' committees in particular services, and initiating joint action will mean that the public service unions will have to widen their view of the role and nature of trade unionism. This includes recognising that their members are also the users of services, and that the level and quality of services are not always secondary to pay and conditions. It also means less reliance on the Labour Party to deal with "political" matters.

More jobs and better pay and conditions can only be achieved in the public services if there is the political support and action to fight for good quality, *public* services under democratic control by workers and users.

It is important how we identify the users of services. A recent Labour Party report "The Responsiveness of Local Services" constantly referred to people as "clients" ("one who employs another professionally as adviser or agent" i.e. a professional expert relationship). Other organisations usually refer to "consumers" or "customers" ("users of products" or "regular patronage of a shop or trader" i.e. an economic/business relationship). It is important to identify them as *users* ("one who uses something for a purpose, ability or power or right to use" i.e. a political relationship). The emphasis in the Labour Party paper is almost entirely on extending "clients' " individual rights, market research, decentralisation and making services more responsive to people. What is needed is *collective* action to *control* services.

● *We need to strengthen trade union organisations in the public services, particularly in local government.* Many areas still don't have joint shop steward committees covering all departments. They are essential to prevent councils playing one department off against another, to unify different trade unions and to co-ordinate action. In London there is an attempt to build a London Local Authority

Trade Union Shop Stewards Committee linking stewards in many boroughs, which aimed, for instance, to build support for the Wandsworth refuse dispute over privatisation. A Tyne and Wear Combine of stewards in Direct Labour Organisations has also helped to get a National Combine of DLO stewards off the ground. Further combines are needed to develop stronger links and support between joint shop stewards committees. Far too much reliance is placed on Joint Consultative Committees with unions and management represented, and on left, Labour controlled authorities and councillors.

We need to build stronger labour movement organisations not as some Alternative Reserve Army for the AES, to be called out on to the streets when parliamentarians get stuck for words, but because they are the roots of the movement, where ideas and real control have to start as actions organised to challenge industrial and finance capital.

Strategies to fight privatisation

A seven-point strategy has been developed by NUPE London Division Local Government Area Committee working in conjunction with SCAT (Services to Community Action and Tenants), and following:

- discussions within the Area Committee and Cuts Sub-committee,
- drawing on the experience and lessons learnt of campaigns in London and elsewhere in fighting privatisation,
- discussions in four half-day educational workshops on privatisation held in London following publication of the broadsheet "Big business Is After Your Job".

The seven elements of the strategy are:

1. *Developing alternative ideas and demands to improve services —* this includes sections on demanding "no privatisation" agreements with Labour-controlled councils, and developing workers' and users' plans.
2. *Education and propaganda —* including preparation of material for the workplace, to users of services and to the wider public, explaining the full effects of privatisation and describing the value and advantages of public services.
3. *Building stronger workplace organisations and links with workers in other boroughs —* through regular

Carlos Augusto (IFL)

Dustmens' demonstration, Wandsworth 10th May 1982; women roadsweepers (TGWU) from Lambeth joined with a one-day solidarity strike.

depot/section/department mass meetings, setting up local authority joint shop stewards committees and links with JSSCs in other areas.

4. *Developing joint action and organising user committees with PTAs, tenants' groups* — why joint action is important and how to develop links with users including some recent examples.

5. *Tactical use of industrial action and negotiating machinery* — including the use of selective strike action, refusing to co-operate with management on various issues, refusal to collect charges and other forms of selective industrial action to strengthen a negotiating position. This must be done in conjunction with other action in order to minimise the alienation of the users of services.

6. *Direct action by workers and users* — including picketing, organising boycotts, occupations and campaigns to improve services — all to strengthen industrial action and build political support.

7. *Counter-offensive against contractors in public services* — covering fighting the preparation of tenders, imposing

conditions on contractors through the implementation of strong Standing Orders, and campaigning to remove existing contractors.

The strategy has been drawn up on the understanding that:

- It is not a shopping list from which you can choose. We believe any campaign against privatisation must involve all seven elements of the strategy although the degree to which each is used will depend on local circumstances. No one tactic will win a struggle against contractors. Success will depend on using these seven strategies in combination.
- It is essential to develop an early warning system to identify the threat of privatisation — you can't wait till contractors are coming through the gate. We have developed the idea of Job Monitoring to help provide an early warning system.
- The contractors are mainly national and multinational companies — they are not local cowboy outfits. These large firms have the resources to put in "loss leader" bids in the anticipation of further contracts later and to spend extravagantly on propaganda, wining and dining.
- Privatisation is a political attack on public services and cannot be fought by traditional trade union action alone.
- It directly affects workers, the services and users and is therefore an increasingly important issue for all sections of the labour movement.
- It cannot be fought by simply defending existing services or adopting defensive tactics — these must be part of a strategy to improve and expand public services and part of a counter offensive against private contractors' existing work with the public services.
- We can't afford and shouldn't try to outbid the contractors — that means getting into a job loss/wage cutting downward spiral. Instead we have to campaign and negotiate for good quality, wide range of services to meet social needs; decent pay, benefits and working conditions; and more worker and user control in running services. Contractors cannot compete on these terms.
- Privatisation can only effectively be fought by joint action both within and outside the work place. It cannot be separated from the fight against the cuts nor the struggle to obtain a decent living wage.

● Constant education and propaganda is needed to expose the contractors, to counter attacks on the public services in the media, and to build public support for public services.

Workers' and users' plans

Workers' and users' plans in the public services can be an important way of developing the much needed alternative ideas and proposals. They can provide the framework in which workers and users can develop their existing and new ideas about what kind of services are wanted and needed and how they can be democratically controlled.

A detailed plan could consist of four main parts covering:

● Investment and resources — finance, labour, materials and other resources needed to improve and expand services, how they could be obtained, training needs, etc.

● Production or service plan — how a particular service could be improved, how it could be reorganised to meet workers' and users' needs.

● Use and organisation — proposals for greater workers' and users' control of services, democratising management, etc.

● Action — what kind of action is needed to get the proposals implemented, how the workers' and users' plan will be used as part of the wider struggle.

The process of drawing up a plan or set of ideas is equally as important as any later set of proposals. A plan is no substitute for basic organising and action within trade unions and the rest of the labour movement. However it can provide workers and users with a means of adding a new dimension to existing campaigns and a new vehicle to assist in organising and encouraging unity.

Workers and users' plans are a means of drawing up negotiating demands i.e. they are not just a collection of "good ideas", but the process of planning and organising can enable workers and users to build confidence, strength and unity to take action to get demands implemented. These ideas and demands will form *part* of the development of both local and national alternative economic, political and social strategies. They are a means of getting the debate about alternative policies broadened out from the current concentration on generalised economic issues.

There is a danger that in the "popularisation" of plans the original concept gets lost, distorted, or absorbed into the state's machinery (see next section). It is therefore essential that we develop a strong set of criteria which can be rigorously applied to test the use, aims and possible benefits of such plans *before* they are initiated. The criteria could include:

- how will they be used to build and strengthen work place organisation, tenants' and users' organisations, and links between the two?
- how will the ideas and proposals be developed into negotiating demands and used as such?
- how will they *add* to existing struggles rather than be a diversion away from them?
- how will education and propaganda form part of the process in developing a "plan" and political support built up for the ideas and demands?
- how can rank and file workers and users retain control of the planning process?

Implications of this strategy for the trade union movement

1. Given the financial resources, diversity of products and services, structure, centralised control and political power of the mainly multinational companies competing for contracts, any effective action by the trade union movement would have to be based on:

- building greater unity and co-operation between the different public sector unions;
- developing links and co-ordination with industrial unions who may have members working in other parts of these companies and have experience of dealing with these companies;
- undertaking more research and analysis of these companies' activities;
- supporting the organisation of joint shop stewards' committees covering different departments in an authority, joint shops stewards' committees covering several councils e.g. London Local Authority Joint Union Shop Stewards' Committee, and combine committees linking up joint shops stewards' committees regionally or nationally e.g. Tyne & Wear DLO Combine and the National DLO Combine.

2. The drawing up of ideas and proposals to improve and expand services and workers' and users' plans will require additional support and assistance from trade unions. The process of

developing such ideas and plans is equally as important as the set of proposals at the end. This support will involve making services available to members and responding quickly to their requests for assistance (technical, organising and campaigning advice) — existing officers and organisers are already over-stretched dealing

St. Mary's Hospital picket.

with pay negotiations, disputes and other trade union work. Public sector trade unions should urgently consider extending their research and education work by developing resource units to carry out this work, to draw on the experience of some of the Labour and Community Resource Centres which have built up considerable experience in this field and to directly support their work.

3. The education of members must play a crucial role in developing strategies to fight privatisation and in developing ideas to improve public servces. The two NUPE education packs on privatisation and the accompanying educational programme could be extended by other unions. The TUC Education Department can play an important role in organising educational workshops which draw together shop stewards from different unions. This educational work should not only help to develop much greater understanding about the threat of privatisation and developing strategies to fight it, but should also provide a stimulus for members to step beyond the traditional economism of jobs, wages and conditions and to see themselves also as the users of services.

There is a need for a range of educational workshops with one- or two-day educationals drawing together the very active and experienced shop stewards to half-day or one-day workshops for branch members in particular localities. Because privatisation is such a fundamental threat there should also be input to other courses run by individual unions and the TUC. This education should not simply be geared to responding to specific threats of privatisation but to prepare members to take action before they are threatened.

4. Developing links, joint action and workers' and users' organisations will also mean having to draw more substantially on the experience of the community action and women's movements both in terms of campaigning/direct action tactics, and building organisation.

Independence from the state

This chapter has argued for a new political strategy by the labour movement for the public services. This must be developed as an independent strategy, avoiding being absorbed into parliamentarism and the local state. For state workers this poses many problems. There is also the need to fight for changes in the proposals now being formulated which a Labour Government might implement e.g. TUC-Labour Party Liaison Committee proposals for Economic Planning and Industrial Democracy which rely heavily on centralised planning, extending trade union representation into state machinery, and gives little recognition for workers' and users' initiatives of the type outlined above.

We have to develop organisation, action and plans *independently* of the state. Workers and users will have to retain this independence — to demand, negotiate and take action to get the state to implement *their* proposals. We don't want an expansion of services under municipal enterprise in which councils simply expand the production of goods and services without changing the way they are produced, run and controlled, or hive-off jobs and services to co-ops outside the public sector.

The response of the local state will obviously vary depending on political control, etc. Where there are currently the greatest opportunities e.g. Sheffield, Greater London Council, West Midlands, there is also the greatest danger of the labour movement's ideas, plans and strategies being incorporated by the state and losing potential and essential gains in the process.

The dangers are:

- *the incorporation of struggle* — getting workers and users involved in planning could be used as a diversion from struggles over pay, conditions, cuts and quality of services.
- *the blurring of ideology* — whose ideas are they? Whose planning? Who's implementing the proposals? A shop stewards' committee wanting to initiate a workers' and users' plan but also wanting the authority to allocate time and resources to develop the plan, may later find the authority claiming "ownership" and credit for any ideas and proposals. Some authorities may well succumb to political pressures for "successes" and therefore push workers and users to forgo the process of planning in order to get quick results.
- limiting the building of organisations — leadership bought off by representation on committees and comfortable meetings within the town hall. There is also the problem of how workers within the state build up relationships with users who are "outside" the state. Users may see workers negotiating and/or co-operating with management and councillors but not see much happening directly in their interests or as a result of their action

or their political support for joint initiatives. There is also the danger of some authorities encouraging participatory popular planning but within existing structures, procedures and controls or setting up new committees without real powers and finance to implement proposals. This may allow individuals more influence but stifle rank and file organising.

- *weakening strategies to gain control of services* — this won't be handed over by management or councillors but will have to be fought for through negotiations, industrial and direct action. An effective system of industrial democracy and greater control in the planning and running of services can only be achieved by building and retaining strong, effective and independent organisations.

Conclusions:
what to do next

Hugo Levie
(TURU, Ruskin College)

A programme for further discussion and research

The examples in the previous sections of this book point out that there is not one pattern of privatisation or of trade union response to it. Clearly there is a concerted Conservative strategy to break down the public sector, but the cases show that the nature and timing of the attacks on jobs and services vary considerably.

The same is true of the trade union reactions. For example, the gas unions held a day of action and joined with other groups opposing the sale of the gas showrooms. Post Office unions initiated a Parliamentary campaign against the British Telecommunications Act. The TGWU advised its members not to buy shares in the management (and bank)-owned National Freight Company. NUPE and SCAT have organised on-the-ground campaigns to publicise the effects of contracting out local authority services.

These differences imply that, as long as Conservative policies predominate, there cannot be one grand strategy dealing with all forms of privatisation.

However, some issues of more general importance to the labour movement stand out from the examples of privatisation. The following points are worthy of much more discussion than they have received so far. They also can be seen as a research programme, where research done by one union or groups of shop stewards can be of great use to others. The points are grouped in three sections: (1) analysing privatisation; (2) strategies against attacks on public services (3) and socialism versus capitalist ideology.

Analysing privatisation

The new private markets and the companies carving them up

In many instances of privatisation there are strong pressures from capitalist enterprises trying to influence exactly what will be privatised and how it will be done. This is certainly true for the undermining of the National Health Service, the privatisation of refuse collection, street cleaning, laundry services, the "liberalisation" of British Telecom. A number of large companies like Grand Met, Trusthouse Forte, Pritchards, BUPA, American Medical International are rapidly moving into the market they helped create themselves.

These advocates of a free market are supposedly all fierce competitors in the areas where they operate. But are they really competing?

That seems unlikely, because they have a strong joint interest in expanding these new markets, i.e. getting local councils and the NHS to put public services out to tender. It may well be that this joint interest is more important than competition between them. What do we know about cartel agreements between these companies? Is there a pattern in which companies bid for certain contracts, for example by region? Is it predictable which company will put in the lowest offer? Are there other links between these companies, like joint directors, joint subsidiaries? For example, do some of the supposed catering competitors engage in joint development of the latest in profitable fast food lines for the school meals market?

Figures on privatisation

Some people feel a need to develop "socialist accounting" as a method to demonstrate the real costs and benefits of privatisation. Clearly they have a point, the efficiency and profitability of public service cannot just be measured in money saved, services cut and jobs lost. All kinds of social factors have to be taken into account:
- the cost to the community of inferior services (refuse collection);
- the opportunity cost of two sets of services: one for the poor another for the rich (NHS and private health clinics);
- the cost of extra unemployment;
- the cost of minimal investment by private contractors who concentrate on immediate returns;
- the existing additional cost of living in rural areas which will be exacerbated by supposedly economic costing of services (telephones and public transport are obvious examples).

However, socialist accounting still needs a lot of development. In the meantime it is dangerous to leave the whole field of figures on moves towards privatisation to "capitalist accountants". Conventional accounting can be used to show up how expensive it will be in a few years time to accept loss leaders now. Conventional accounting can be used to prove the fallacy of a comparison between refuse collection by the council and private contractors. If, for example, capital costs are left out on the contractor's side, but included heftily on the council side of the comparison. Or if the figures produced by the advocates of privatisation give an unreal picture by forgetting that the privatised services will be of a lower standard, thereby precluding a straight financial comparison. Perhaps it would be impossible to use conventional accounting, to convince Tory controlled councils, although it has been known to make them uneasy. It certainly could be used to show to the people in the area concerned that they will have to pay for privatisation, either in increased rates in the future, or in lost services, or both. Furthermore reduced wages paid to contractors' employees will be reflected in lower spending and a drop in the general standard of living in the area concerned, which will affect everyone.

The role of management consultants

Management consultants are known to line up at the Department of the Environment to sell their own form of hatchet investigation that could be used to hive off, contract out, or otherwise undermine, local public services. Who are these consultants and how do they work? Are they linked to the companies that pick up the privatised services? How far do these consultants use standard packages meant to help justify decisions already taken? How much are they paid? Are their reports available to all councillors and to the workers and trade unions involved? Some more information about the consultants who prepare the ground for attacks on public services probably would be very helpful to the workers and trade union representatives involved.

Strategies for privatisation

It seems clear that the Government has stepped up its concerted campaign for privatisation since the beginning of 1982. The forms that privatisation can take vary, and, for instance, in the case of the gas showrooms and British Telecom, the Government has shown considerable flexibility in its plans. It would be naïve however, to suppose that their is no planning; potential victims would be helped by more systematic analysis of Tory strategies for privatisation (timing, the use of carrots and sticks, the use of law, responsiveness to the wishes of the companies that would benefit). Such analysis probably would also show that in many cases privatisation is not just a specific answer by a local council to specific cuts demanded or imposed by central government. Many Conservatives have accepted privatisation as an aim and pursue it even if they realise that in the end it will be more expensive than keeping services public. Particularly since the Tories took office in 1979, privatisation increasingly has become a policy in its own right and is being prepared as a major plank of the Tory manifesto for the next General Elections. To Conservatives at different levels of Government, both national and local, privatisation has become appreciated as a vehicle for their own interests. At least one majority group of Tory County Councillors is known to have set up its own "privatisation working party". Another reason why privatisation has jelled since 1979 is that Conservative business interests have had their own reasons for assisting the Tories in the development of their policies.

Strategies against attacks on public services
Arguments, action and alliances

The examples in previous sections show that a trade union strategy against privatisation will contain elements under one or more of the following headings:
- arguments against privatisation;
- industrial action to stop privatisation;
- building alliances against privatisation with other interest groups.

It seems likely that strategies that are well developed under each of these headings stand the best chance of blocking privatisation moves. The history of the last three years indicates however, that most campaigns against privatisation are under-developed in one or more of these three areas — not through lack of trying, but because of the major problems that exist in the development of counter-arguments, industrial action or wider alliances against privatisation.

Arguments against privatisation

The examples of privatisation show that nowadays nobody

(workers, consumers, certainly not the media) can be expected to help defend a public service for the mere reason that it is public. The moral argument that public is better will not convince sufficient people. More precise arguments are needed for each individual case to show people how privatisation will affect them. One lesson from the recent history of privatisation is that arguments against privatisation often are not there, waiting to be used. On the contrary, they have to be developed carefully, perhaps for different audiences, like the workforce, consumer bodies, the local or national media. It may be necessary to do some research to prepare these arguments. It is clearly important that this work is started now, for all public services which may be future victims of privatisation. In fact, it has become very hard to think of any public service which doesn't fall into this category.

Different lines of argument may have to be pursued, for example:

What will go wrong after privatisation?

Analysis of the plans for privatisation may show clearly:
- that the service will *deteriorate;*
- that it will become more *expensive* (now or in a few years);
- that it will affect the *local community* involved (higher unemployment, lower wages);

Arguments that equalise public services with progress are no longer sufficient.

- that the *quality of life of producers and consumers* of the service will suffer (for example, if school meals become expensive or stop altogether, parents will have to make up packed lunches; if public transport deteriorates people without their own transport will have to travel less, or to spend more time travelling or to pay more for alternatives).

Apart from trying to predict what could go wrong if a specific public service was privatised, trade unionists could also help themselves and each other by monitoring in practice what did happen after privatisation. Real stories of what went wrong may be the best argument to convince people of the disadvantage of privatisation.

What is efficiency?

If the Government attacks jobs in the civil service in a so-called campaign against "waste and inefficiency" (see chapter 8) which trade unionist wants to be forced into a position where people think that he, or she is in favour of waste and inefficiency? Since the answer is 'Nobody', it is a matter of developing arguments against false definitions of efficiency. This is clearly a difficult area, firstly because it requires a detailed analysis of the figures for — and against — privatisation. More importantly, because we want to convince people who are not yet convinced of the disadvantages to them if the same service was done privately. It may be necessary therefore to admit that as it is, the service is far from efficient and could be improved in many ways. In other words, it may be contentious but we have to develop our own definition of efficiency and our own ideas for improving public services. The experience of the Society of Civil and Public Servants shows that this is a difficult process especially for people who work in services that are immediately under attack.

Industrial Action?

What are the weapons of public sector workers trying to defend their services and jobs? There are three problems in relation to strike action:

— it may not affect the employer directly, if no sales or customers are lost. (This argument is less true for public transport and utilities);

— it is not directly conducive to forging an alliance with the consumers, because they are often hit much more than the employers;

— it may make it easier, not harder, for the employer to close the service or privatise it.

Factory occupation has been developed by private sector workers as a weapon against closure. Although success is not guaranteed, occupation as an ultimate weapon has some clear advantages over strike action. Production can go on and it becomes harder, not easier, to close the place. Is it possible to think of forms of action in the public sector which affect consumers less and the employer more? Some examples already exist: continuing the bus service, but not collecting the fares; helping the "customer", but leaving the administrative work.

Another form of defensive action is to fight for measures that will make it more difficult for local councils to hive off public services, for example protective clauses in the council's standing orders.

Building alliances

The fight against privatisation of the gas showrooms points to the importance of an alliance between producers and consumers. In other cases, it may be more difficult to forge such an alliance. For example, there may be a strong lobby of companies pushing for privatisation like the telecommunication equipment concerns who lobbied very hard for the "liberalisation" of British Telecom. Another difficulty in the forging of alliances may be that whilst the private enterprise that will be affected by privatisation may be successful in co-ordinating their campaign for privatisation, individual consumers often are not that well organised.

A third problem may be that certain groups of workers could be convinced that they will benefit from privatisation. For example, because they work for a private concern that will see its market enhanced. Or perhaps because they work for a viable establishment in the public sector which would benefit if its investment plans were no longer artifically curtailed by the Public Sector Borrowing Requirement.

Not many workers will be able to keep their services public

without widespread support. The lessons from previous cases is clearly that public sector will have to work now on the alliances it will need in coming years. If it comes to a specific push for privatisation, the workers involved will mostly have to depend on existing alliances, and often that is not enough.

Underlying this question of alliances are obviously important and far-reaching questions that are crucial to the general direction of the Labour movement.

NUPE section of a march for jobs organised by the Labour Party, Cardiff July 1981.

Socialism versus capitalist ideology

Producers and consumers

Capitalist ideology emphasises individualism. All people are equal and have equal chances, some are more successful than others in the struggle for life; that it is their own, individual good — or bad — luck. Socialists know this is nonsense, positive action is needed against existing, enormous inequalities and for a better, more equal world. Socialists also know that this positive action will only happen if we do not accept the capitalist preference for individualism and work together. Trade unions are supposed to be organisations of workers, working together against inequality. The fight against privatisation brings a particular problem to the fore: where are the organisations of consumers that will fight against a deterioration of services? Users' councils do exist for most of the nationalised industries and utilities, but at present they only scratch the surface of what needs doing, and they are not democratically constituted. Have socialists a long time ago fallen into the trap of capitalist ideology, which tells us that consumers are all individuals making individual choices how they are going to spend their "personal disposable income"? Is there still a chance for workers in the public sector to build alliances with users of their services?

Cross-subsidy or redistribution?

One of the principles of parliamentary socialist thinking since 1945 has been redistribution of wealth and income. Perhaps this is the most important form of positive action underlying the parliamentary socialist concept of the welfare state. The present government is actively against equalising wealth and income. What is even more disturbing is that the political and moral desirability of redistribution does not seem to be anchored in the minds of the great majority of the population. People who rent a council house pay for the mortgage interest relief received by home-owners and their is no outcry against it. Private telephone users pay in real terms more than businesses and the resistance is minimal. Cross-subsidisation is the new taboo, the positive principle of redistribution has been forgotten. But cross-subsidisation is common in the private sector. Contractors putting in low tenders to win a local authority service are clearly cross-subsidising their loss leading offer. Why should the cross-subsidisation be taboo in the public sector? Why should the poor pay as much for a particular service as the rich?

In the past, Labour and the trade unions have relied perhaps too much on redistribution as a way to change society. But to drop it altogether as a principle and to start sharing the Conservatives' dislike of so-called cross-subsidies seems a bit too crude.

Wider share ownership or pension power?

The need to look a bit closer at the companies carving up public services has already been mentioned. But who owns these companies? How far are workers' own pension funds involved? Do we let potential pension power go by default, instead of using it to stop privatisation, or at least to force the companies involved not to break into existing services by proposing unrealistic loss leaders?

The Tories and their City advisors seem to be more clever. They are aware of the potential power of concentrated ownership in the hands of pension funds. What, for them, is a better safeguard against the use of that power by us, to further our aims, than "wider share ownership"? All workers at the National Freight Company (NFC) buy a share in the company and management increase their control. First, they own more shares anyway, particularly in combination with the banks. Second, if they attack one group of workers, "for the greater good of the company as a whole", the other workers/share owners will have split loyalties. In the particular case of the NFC, the situation is not that bleak since the TGWU has been successful in its recommendation to its members at NFC not to buy shares. But the Tory principle of "wider share ownership" certainly has not been defeated. What will happen in the case of British Telecom, or in case of privatisation of (parts of) British Airways? Does experience not show that "wider share ownership" means that the power is in the hands of a few large shareholders whilst a large number of small shareholders have a completely passive role? Does not the issue of privatisation force workers and trade unions in the public sector to increase the time and energy they spend on increasing their control over their own pension funds and their investment policies?

What do we expect from the state?

There is a parliamentary socialist tradition that maintains that the state is neutral. Is it still possible to hold that position? Dexter Whitfield and Dave Hall argue in their contribution (chapter 9) that workers in the public sector should not expect too much from the state, not even from Labour-controlled local councils. Are there really still alternatives to this point of view, which basically takes issue with the tradition of the neutral state.

Is it realistic to expect that Labour councils or even better, a Labour Government, will be able to bring back the old public services for us? There are some clear lessons that we can draw from the lack of resistance the Tories have met in their privatisation campaign. Can't we start thinking about alternatives to a welfare state that looks after passive individuals? There are no easy answers but should we not try to give the "public" in public services a new meaning: services for, controlled by, and accountable to the people? Our strategies would become more convincing if we countered the Conservative ideology of privatisation with proposals for really *public* services.